Cryptocurrency Made Simple

A 10-Step Guide to Understanding Digital Currency

Bruno Steele

Contents

Introduction

Welcome to a journey that will transform how you understand and interact with the future of money. Like many of you, I remember the first time I heard about Bitcoin - a digital currency that promised to revolutionize our financial system. Initially, it seemed complex, perhaps even a bit intimidating. That's exactly why I wrote this book.

Through years of exploring, trading, and teaching others about cryptocurrency, I've discovered that the key to understanding this revolutionary technology isn't in mastering complex technical jargon or becoming a coding expert. Instead, it's about grasping the fundamental principles that make digital currencies work and learning how to navigate this new financial landscape safely and confidently.

In the pages that follow, we'll embark on a carefully structured journey through the world of cryptocurrency. We'll start with the basics - understanding how money itself has evolved from ancient times to the digital age. We'll explore the revolutionary technology behind cryptocurrencies, learn how to secure and manage digital assets, and develop strategies for making informed investment decisions.

But this isn't just another technical manual. Through real stories and practical examples, we'll see how cryptocurrency is already changing lives and reshaping our world. You'll meet people like Sienna, an archaeologist who discovered fascinating parallels between ancient coins and modern digital currencies, and Curtis, whose careful attention to security protocols saved him from a sophisticated crypto scam.

Whether you're completely new to cryptocurrency or have some experience but want to deepen your understanding, this book is designed to meet you where you are. We'll tackle essential questions like: How does blockchain technology actually work? What makes Bitcoin different from traditional currency? How can you safely buy and store cryptocurrencies? What are the risks and opportunities in this emerging market?

My goal is to empower you with knowledge and practical skills to confidently participate in the digital economy. The cryptocurrency revolution isn't just about technology - it's about creating new opportunities for financial inclusion and innovation. By the time you finish this book, you'll have the foundation needed to understand, evaluate, and engage with cryptocurrencies in ways that align with your personal financial goals.

As we begin this journey together, remember that every expert was once a beginner. The crypto space is constantly evolving, and maintaining a mindset of curiosity and continuous learning is key to success. Let's take that first step together into the fascinating world of digital currency, where innovation meets opportunity, and the future of finance is being written one block at a time.

Let's make the complex simple and the intimidating accessible. Welcome to Crypto Made Simple: A 10-Step Guide to Understanding Digital Currency.

Chapter One

The Evolution of Money: From Barter to Bitcoin

Money, in its various forms, has been humanity's most transformative invention for facilitating trade and storing value. As we trace its evolution from shells and precious metals to digital bits and bytes, we uncover a fascinating story of human ingenuity and adaptation that continues to shape our world. This fascinating journey through monetary history reveals how each innovation in currency has fundamentally transformed human civilization and commerce. From the earliest days of bartering goods and services to the complex digital networks that power today's cryptocurrency transactions, we can trace a clear path of evolving needs and solutions in how humans exchange value.

The concept of money itself has been remarkably consistent in its core functions - serving as a medium of exchange, store of value, and unit of account. Yet the forms it takes have transformed dramatically as societies have grown more complex and interconnected. Understanding this evolution provides crucial context for grasping cryptocurrency's revolutionary potential.

This reality was beautifully illustrated recently when Sienna, a young archaeologist, was excavating an ancient marketplace in Greece and discovered a collection of silver drachmas dating back to the 5th century BCE. As she carefully cleaned each coin, she couldn't help but draw parallels between these ancient pieces of currency and the cryptocurrency she had recently started investing in. The drachmas in her hands had once represented a revolutionary standardization of trade - trusted, portable, and valuable. They solved the same fundamental problems that Bitcoin addresses today: the need for reliable, transferable value.

While documenting her find, Sienna used her phone to check her crypto wallet, marveling at how the basic concept of money had evolved from these physical coins to digital assets she could access with a fingertip. The ancient coins and her digital wallet, separated by millennia of monetary evolution, shared the same core purpose - enabling human commerce and cooperation. This realization helped Sienna understand that cryptocurrency wasn't just a technological innovation, but rather the next logical step in money's long evolutionary journey.

As we explore this evolution, we'll discover how each major monetary innovation – from standardized coins to paper money to digital transactions – has emerged in response to specific economic and social needs. We'll see how cryptocurrency represents a natural progression in this journey, offering solutions to modern challenges of international commerce, financial inclusion, and the digital economy.

In this chapter, we'll trace money's transformative path from its earliest forms through to today's cryptocurrencies, examining how each development has built upon previous innovations while addressing new challenges. This historical context is essential for understanding not just where cryptocurrency came from, but where it might be leading us in the future of global finance.

The Origins of Trade: Understanding Barter Systems and Early Forms of Money

Long before the invention of coins or paper money, humans developed sophisticated systems of trade through bartering – the direct exchange of goods and services. This fundamental economic practice emerged around 6000 BC in Mesopotamia, where tribes first established formal systems for trading essential items like food, weapons, and crafts. As human societies grew more complex and interconnected, these early trading systems laid the groundwork for all future monetary innovations.

The Phoenicians played a pivotal role in expanding and refining barter trade beyond local regions. Their strategic coastal location and access to valuable cedar and fir forests enabled them to establish extensive trading networks across oceans and between distant cities. They would exchange timber and crafted goods with Mesopotamians for foodstuffs grown along the Nile River, demonstrating how even without currency, complex international commerce could flourish.

Certain commodities gained particular significance in these early trading systems. Salt became so valuable that Roman soldiers were sometimes compensated with it, while items like weapons, spices, tea, and wine served as common trading goods across different societies. The Babylonians further refined these trading practices, developing more sophisticated methods for determining fair exchange values between different types of goods.

One fascinating variation that emerged was the "silent barter," where traders who spoke different languages or were wary of direct contact could still conduct business. This practice demonstrated human ingenuity in overcoming communication barriers to facilitate commerce. As trading networks expanded, the limitations of pure barter systems became increasingly apparent – the need for a coincidence of wants (both parties having exactly what the other desires) made trade increasingly cumbersome.

These limitations eventually led to the development of intermediate commodities that could serve as widely accepted mediums of exchange. Items like shells, beads, and precious metals began to function as proto-currencies, bridging the gap between pure barter and standardized money systems. This evolution wasn't just about convenience – it represented a fundamental shift in how humans conceived of value and conducted commerce.

The principles established during this early period of economic development continue to influence modern financial innovations. Just as early traders sought more efficient ways to exchange value, today's cryptocurrency systems aim to create new solutions for value transfer in our digital age. Understanding these origins helps us appreciate how each monetary innovation, from shells to silver coins to digital tokens, builds upon humanity's ongoing quest to facilitate trade and cooperation.

The transition from direct bartering to using intermediate commodities marked a crucial step in monetary evolution. These early forms of "money" needed to be portable, durable, divisible, and widely accepted – characteristics that would later define successful currencies throughout history. This shift fundamentally transformed human civilization by enabling more complex economic relationships and laying the foundation for modern financial systems.

The Rise of Standardized Currency: From Precious Metals to Fiat Money

The emergence of standardized currency marked a pivotal transformation in human civilization, fundamentally changing how societies conducted trade and stored wealth. Around 640 BCE, in what is now Henan Province, China, the world's oldest known coin minting facility began producing standardized spade coins. This revolutionary development represented one of humanity's first attempts to create a regulated, uniform monetary system that could facilitate trade more efficiently than the variable commodity currencies that preceded it.

The introduction of standardized metal coins solved many of the practical challenges that had limited earlier forms of trade. Unlike bartering or using inconsistent commodity currencies, coins provided a universally recognized value standard that dramatically accelerated commercial activities. This standardization enabled merchants to conduct transactions more quickly and confidently, knowing that the currency they received held consistent value across different markets and regions.

As trade networks expanded and transactions grew larger, the practical limitations of metal currencies became increasingly apparent. Carrying large quantities of metal coins proved cumbersome and risky for merchants conducting substantial business. This challenge led to another revolutionary monetary innovation in 7th century China - the introduction of paper currency. This development marked a crucial step toward more sophisticated financial systems, offering advantages in portability, storage, and transaction efficiency.

The widespread adoption of paper currency necessitated new systems of trust and verification. Banking institutions emerged to facilitate these monetary exchanges, and innovative financial instruments like letters of credit became common practice. These developments allowed merchants to conduct business across vast distances without physically transporting valuable metals, significantly reducing risks and costs associated with trade.

The relationship between precious metals and paper currency reached its most structured form with the implementation of the gold standard. Under this system, governments backed their paper money with equivalent amounts of gold reserves, providing a tangible foundation for currency value. This arrangement reached its apex with the Bretton Woods Agreement after World War II, which established a system where participating countries pegged their currencies to the US dollar, which was in turn backed by gold at $35 per troy ounce.

A monumental shift occurred in 1971 when the United States ended the dollar's fixed conversion rate to gold, effectively terminating the Bretton Woods system. This decision marked the transition to the modern era of fiat currency - money that derives its value not from physical commodities but from government declaration and public trust. This transformation gave central banks unprecedented flexibility in managing national economies through monetary policy, while also introducing new challenges in maintaining currency stability.

The evolution from precious metals to fiat money represents more than just a change in the physical form of currency - it reflects humanity's growing sophistication in understanding and managing economic value. Each innovation, from standardized coins to paper money to fiat currency, has built upon previous developments while addressing new challenges in facilitating trade and storing value. This evolutionary process continues today as we witness the emergence of digital currencies, suggesting that our journey of monetary innovation is far from complete.

Digital Revolution: The Emergence of Cryptocurrency and Bitcoin

The dawn of digital currency marks one of the most significant innovations in monetary history since the invention of paper money. In 2008, amidst a global financial crisis that shook faith in traditional banking systems, an anonymous figure using the pseudonym Satoshi Nakamoto published a revolutionary white paper titled "Bitcoin: A Peer-to-Peer Electronic Cash System." This document outlined a groundbreaking vision for a decentralized digital currency that would operate without the need for intermediaries like banks or governments.

The roots of this innovation stretch back to the early 1980s when American cryptographer David Chaum introduced the concept of "ecash," a form of cryptographically secure electronic money. This early work laid the foundation for future developments in digital currency. Throughout the 1990s, the Cypherpunk movement championed the use of cryptography to promote privacy and individual autonomy in financial transactions, creating an intellectual environment that would eventually nurture Bitcoin's development.

On January 3, 2009, the Bitcoin network officially launched with the mining of the first block, known as the genesis block. This moment marked the beginning of a new era in financial technology. Just days later, Nakamoto released Bitcoin's open-source code, enabling anyone to participate in the system. The first real-world transaction occurred when Nakamoto sent 10 bitcoins to Hal Finney, a noted cryptographer and early supporter of the project.

Bitcoin introduced several revolutionary concepts that would fundamentally change how we think about money. Its decentralized ledger, known as the blockchain, eliminated the need for traditional financial intermediaries by creating a transparent, immutable record of all transactions. The proof-of-work consensus mechanism ensured network security through computational work performed by miners, while the fixed supply cap of 21 million bitcoins created digital scarcity, mimicking precious metals' inherent value proposition.

The success of Bitcoin catalyzed an explosion of innovation in the cryptocurrency space. By 2011, alternative cryptocurrencies began emerging, each introducing unique features or improvements. Namecoin attempted to decentralize Internet domain name registration, while Litecoin implemented a different hashing algorithm for faster transaction processing. Peercoin introduced proof-of-stake as an energy-efficient alternative to Bitcoin's proof-of-work system.

The implications of this digital revolution extend far beyond the realm of finance. Cryptocurrency represents a fundamental shift in how we conceptualize and transfer value in the digital age. It challenges traditional notions of monetary sovereignty and raises important questions about the future of financial systems. As Kim Dotcom, the Internet entrepreneur, observed, "Bitcoin is an exciting development, it might lead to a world currency. I think over the next decade it will grow to become one of the most important ways to pay for things and transfer assets."

The real-world adoption of cryptocurrency was perhaps best illustrated by what is now known as "Bitcoin Pizza Day." On May 22, 2010, Laszlo Hanyecz completed the first known commercial transaction using Bitcoin, paying 10,000 bitcoins for two pizzas. This transaction not only demonstrated Bitcoin's potential as a medium of exchange but also marked the beginning of its journey from a theoretical concept to a practical currency.

As we continue to witness the evolution of digital currency, it's clear that the emergence of cryptocurrency represents more than just a technological innovation – it's a paradigm shift in how we think about money, value, and financial sovereignty. The principles of decentralization, cryptographic security, and peer-to-peer transactions that Bitcoin introduced continue to influence the development of new financial technologies and challenge our traditional understanding of monetary systems. As we conclude this exploration of money's evolution, from its humble beginnings in ancient markets to the cutting-edge world of cryptocurrency, several key insights emerge. The journey from barter systems to digital currencies reveals not just technological advancement, but humanity's constant drive to create more efficient, secure, and accessible means of exchanging value.

Through Sienna's story of discovering ancient drachmas while managing her crypto wallet, we witnessed how the fundamental purpose of money remains unchanged across millennia. Whether carved in metal or encoded in blockchain, currency continues to serve its essential functions as a medium of exchange, store of value, and unit of account. The tools and technologies may evolve, but the core needs they address remain remarkably consistent.

The emergence of standardized currencies marked a pivotal moment in human civilization, solving the inherent limitations of barter systems and enabling more complex economic relationships. This standardization laid the groundwork for the sophisticated financial systems we rely on today. The transition to paper money and eventually fiat currency demonstrated how trust and social agreement could transform intrinsically valueless materials into powerful economic tools.

Now, as we stand at the threshold of a new monetary era, cryptocurrency represents the latest chapter in this ongoing story of innovation. It addresses modern challenges of globalization, digital commerce, and financial inclusion while building upon centuries of monetary evolution. The principles that made ancient coins valuable - scarcity, portability, durability, and universal acceptance - find new expression in digital forms.

Perhaps most importantly, this chapter reminds us that monetary innovation isn't just about technology - it's about people finding better ways to cooperate, trade, and create value together. As we look toward the future of digital currency, understanding this historical context helps us appreciate both the revolutionary potential of cryptocurrency and its place in money's continuing evolution.

As we move forward in our exploration of cryptocurrency, remember that we're not just learning about a new technology - we're participating in the next phase of humanity's ongoing quest to create more effective tools for exchange and cooperation. The principles we've examined in this chapter will serve as a foundation for understanding the more technical aspects of cryptocurrency that we'll explore in the chapters ahead.

Chapter Two

Blockchain Fundamentals: Understanding the Digital Backbone

Imagine a digital chain of information so secure and transparent that it revolutionizes how we track, verify, and exchange value in the modern world. At its core, blockchain technology represents one of the most significant innovations in record-keeping since the invention of double-entry bookkeeping centuries ago. Like the invention of the printing press centuries ago, blockchain technology represents a fundamental shift in how we record, verify and exchange information. This innovative system combines cryptography, distributed computing, and game theory principles to create an immutable, transparent ledger that can track virtually any type of transaction or data exchange.

To truly grasp blockchain's transformative potential, we need to break down its core components into digestible pieces. Think of blockchain as a digital chain of blocks, where each block contains a list of verified transactions. These blocks are linked together using sophisticated mathematical functions, creating an unbreakable chain of information that becomes more secure with each new addition.

During a cryptocurrency workshop I attended, Jack, a skeptical software developer, challenged the host about blockchain's practical applications. He argued that traditional databases could handle most tasks just fine. To help him understand, a simple exercise was created where workshop participants acted as nodes in a network, passing around a ledger and validating transactions. Each person had to agree on changes before they became final. When someone tried to alter a previous entry, the group quickly caught the discrepancy. Jack's eyes lit up as he witnessed firsthand how the system's distributed nature created both transparency and security. By the end of the exercise, he not only understood blockchain's unique value proposition but became one of its most enthusiastic advocates in the group. This hands-on demonstration showed how blockchain's seemingly complex principles could be understood through practical experience, transforming technical skepticism into informed appreciation.

In this chapter, we'll explore the fundamental building blocks of blockchain technology, including distributed ledger technology, consensus mechanisms, and the cryptographic principles that ensure data integrity. We'll examine how these elements work together to create a system that's revolutionizing not just finance, but industries ranging from supply chain management to healthcare. By understanding these core concepts, you'll be better equipped to evaluate blockchain applications and make informed decisions about cryptocurrency investments.

While the technical aspects of blockchain might seem daunting at first, remember that every revolutionary technology - from electricity to the internet - started as a complex concept that eventually became part of our daily lives. The key is to approach the learning process step by step, building a solid foundation of understanding that will serve you well in your cryptocurrency journey.

Distributed Ledger Technology: The Foundation of Blockchain

At the heart of blockchain technology lies a revolutionary system called Distributed Ledger Technology (DLT). This innovative approach to record-keeping fundamentally changes how we store, share, and verify information across networks. Unlike traditional databases that rely on central authorities, DLT spreads identical copies of a ledger across multiple computers or nodes in a network, creating a system that is both transparent and highly resistant to tampering.

To understand DLT, imagine a shared spreadsheet that exists simultaneously on thousands of computers. When someone makes a change to this spreadsheet, all copies update automatically, but only after the majority of participants agree that the change is valid. This consensus-based approach eliminates the need for intermediaries while ensuring the integrity of the data. Each participant maintains their own copy of the ledger, creating a system that is both decentralized and highly resilient to failure or manipulation.

The power of DLT lies in its unique combination of security features. Through sophisticated cryptography, each transaction or piece of information is digitally signed and verified before being added to the ledger. Once recorded, this information becomes permanent and unchangeable, creating an immutable record that can be trusted by all participants. This immutability, combined with the transparent nature of the system, makes DLT particularly valuable for applications requiring high levels of trust and verification.

While blockchain represents the most well-known implementation of DLT, it's important to understand that not all distributed ledgers use blockchain architecture. Some systems employ alternative structures like Directed Acyclic

Graphs (DAGs) or Hashgraph technology. However, they all share the fundamental principles of decentralization, consensus-based validation, and cryptographic security.

The practical applications of DLT extend far beyond cryptocurrency. Financial institutions use this technology to streamline cross-border payments and reduce transaction costs. Supply chain managers employ DLT to track products from origin to destination with unprecedented transparency. Even government agencies are exploring DLT for secure voting systems and digital identity verification.

Perhaps most importantly, DLT addresses one of the fundamental challenges in digital transactions: the double-spending problem. By maintaining a synchronized record across all participants, the system ensures that digital assets can't be duplicated or spent multiple times. This breakthrough has profound implications for digital finance and forms the foundation for trustworthy cryptocurrency transactions.

The security of DLT comes from its distributed nature. Unlike traditional systems where attacking a central database could compromise the entire network, DLT requires potential attackers to simultaneously compromise multiple nodes – a task that becomes exponentially more difficult as the network grows. This resilience, combined with cryptographic protection, makes DLT one of the most secure methods for recording and sharing sensitive information.

As we continue to explore blockchain technology, understanding DLT provides crucial context for how these systems maintain security, ensure transparency, and enable trustless transactions. This foundation will help you better appreciate the revolutionary potential of cryptocurrency and blockchain applications in our increasingly digital world.

Consensus Mechanisms and Network Security

The backbone of blockchain's security and reliability lies in its consensus mechanisms - sophisticated protocols that enable a network of computers to agree on the state of a distributed ledger without central authority oversight. These mechanisms serve as the digital equivalent of a democratic voting system, where participants collectively validate and verify transactions to maintain the integrity of the blockchain.

Consensus mechanisms solve a fundamental challenge in decentralized systems: how to ensure all participants agree on the same version of truth without trusting each other. This is achieved through carefully designed protocols that incentivize honest behavior while making malicious actions prohibitively expensive or technically infeasible. The most well-known consensus mechanism, Proof of Work (PoW), requires participants called miners to solve complex mathematical puzzles, consuming significant computational power to validate transactions and create new blocks.

As blockchain technology has evolved, more energy-efficient alternatives have emerged. Proof of Stake (PoS) selects validators based on the amount of cryptocurrency they're willing to lock up as collateral, significantly reducing energy consumption while maintaining security. This approach has gained prominence with major cryptocurrencies adopting it to address environmental concerns while preserving decentralization.

The security of these consensus mechanisms relies on both technical and economic factors. In PoW systems, the massive computational power required to control the network makes attacks extremely costly. PoS systems create security through economic incentives - validators risk losing their staked assets if they attempt to manipulate the system. This combination of technical barriers and financial deterrents helps maintain the network's integrity.

These mechanisms also incorporate sophisticated defenses against common threats. For instance, they prevent double-spending attacks by ensuring that the entire network agrees on transaction order and validity. Sybil attacks, where malicious actors create multiple fake identities, are thwarted by making network participation computationally or financially expensive.

The automated nature of consensus mechanisms eliminates the need for trust in intermediaries. All participants can independently verify transactions and the current state of the network, creating transparency while maintaining security. Once consensus is achieved and data is recorded on the blockchain, it becomes practically impossible to alter, ensuring the immutability of records.

Fault tolerance is another crucial aspect of consensus mechanisms. Well-designed protocols continue functioning even if some participants act maliciously or go offline. This resilience ensures the network remains operational and secure under various adverse conditions, from technical failures to deliberate attacks.

As blockchain technology continues to evolve, new consensus mechanisms are being developed to address specific needs and use cases. These innovations focus on optimizing the balance between security, scalability, and energy efficiency. Some protocols combine elements from different mechanisms to create hybrid solutions that leverage the strengths of multiple approaches while minimizing their weaknesses.

Understanding consensus mechanisms is crucial for anyone involved in cryptocurrency, as they form the foundation of trust in these decentralized systems. While the technical details may be complex, the basic principle remains simple: creating a system where participants can agree on the validity of transactions without requiring trust in any central authority or each other.

Smart Contracts and Decentralized Applications

Smart contracts represent one of blockchain technology's most revolutionary features, fundamentally changing how we create and execute agreements in the digital age. These self-executing digital contracts automatically enforce predefined rules and conditions without requiring intermediaries, bringing unprecedented automation and transparency to various transactions and processes.

To understand smart contracts, imagine a digital vending machine programmed with unbreakable rules. When you insert the correct amount of money and make a selection, the machine automatically delivers your chosen item - no human intervention required. Smart contracts work similarly but can handle far more complex transactions, from automated loan payments to sophisticated insurance claims processing.

The true power of smart contracts becomes evident when we examine their role in enabling decentralized applications (DApps). These innovative applications run on blockchain networks rather than centralized servers, creating systems that are both transparent and resistant to manipulation. DApps leverage smart contracts to automate complex processes while maintaining security and trust through the underlying blockchain infrastructure.

Smart contracts and DApps work together to create entirely new possibilities for digital interaction and value exchange. For example, decentralized exchanges use smart contracts to enable direct peer-to-peer trading of cryptocurrencies without traditional intermediaries. Supply chain management systems employ smart contracts to automatically track and verify product movements, ensuring transparency and authenticity at every step.

However, it's crucial to understand both the benefits and limitations of these technologies. While smart contracts can significantly reduce costs and eliminate intermediaries, they also require careful programming and thorough security audits. The immutable nature of blockchain means that once deployed, smart contract code cannot be altered - making initial security and accuracy paramount.

The evolution of smart contracts and DApps continues to drive innovation across industries. From decentralized finance platforms that automate lending and borrowing to blockchain-based games that provide true digital asset ownership, these technologies are reshaping how we think about digital interactions and value exchange.

Security considerations play a vital role in smart contract and DApp development. The industry learned valuable lessons from early incidents, particularly The DAO (Decentralized Autonomous Organization) event in 2016, which highlighted the critical importance of rigorous code auditing and security testing. Today, developers implement multiple layers of security measures and extensive testing protocols before deploying smart contracts.

As these technologies mature, they're finding applications far beyond cryptocurrency. Voting systems, supply chain management, insurance processing, and countless other sectors are exploring how smart contracts and DApps can streamline operations and reduce costs. This expansion demonstrates the transformative potential of these technologies in creating more efficient, transparent, and automated systems across various industries.

The accessibility of smart contracts and DApps continues to improve as development tools and platforms evolve. Modern platforms provide user-friendly interfaces that abstract away much of the underlying complexity, making these technologies more accessible to developers and end-users alike. This democratization of access is crucial for the widespread adoption of blockchain technology.

Looking ahead, the combination of smart contracts and DApps promises to revolutionize how we conduct business, manage assets, and interact in the digital world. As these technologies continue to evolve and mature, they're likely to become an increasingly integral part of our digital infrastructure, enabling new forms of collaboration and value exchange that were previously impossible. As we conclude our exploration of blockchain fundamentals, it's worth reflecting on the transformative potential this technology holds. From distributed ledger technology to smart contracts and consensus mechanisms, we've uncovered the building blocks that make blockchain a revolutionary force in our digital world.

Thinking back to Jack's journey from skeptic to advocate during our workshop, we can see how understanding blockchain's core principles transforms perception. His experience mirrors that of many professionals who initially question blockchain's value proposition but come to appreciate its unique capabilities once they grasp the fundamental concepts. The distributed nature of the system, combined with its cryptographic security and consensus mechanisms, creates something truly revolutionary – a trustless system that paradoxically builds trust through transparency and mathematical certainty.

The practical applications of blockchain technology extend far beyond cryptocurrency. While Bitcoin may have been blockchain's first successful implementation, the underlying technology's potential reaches into virtually every sector of our economy. From supply chain management to healthcare records, from voting systems to financial services, blockchain's ability to create immutable, transparent records while maintaining security and privacy opens doors to innovations we're only beginning to imagine.

Yet, understanding blockchain fundamentals is just the first step in your cryptocurrency journey. Armed with this knowledge, you're now better equipped to evaluate different blockchain projects, understand their value propositions, and make informed decisions about potential investments. Remember that like any transformative technology, blockchain continues to evolve, with new consensus mechanisms, smart contract capabilities, and applications emerging regularly.

As we move forward to explore more specific aspects of cryptocurrency in the coming chapters, keep these fundamental concepts in mind. They form the foundation upon which all cryptocurrency innovations are built, an understanding of them will serve as your compass in navigating the exciting but sometimes complex world of digital assets.

Remember, blockchain technology represents more than just a new way to record transactions - it's a paradigm shift in how we think about trust, transparency, and value exchange in the digital age. With this foundation in place, you're ready to explore the practical aspects of cryptocurrency investment and participation in the blockchain ecosystem.

Chapter Three

Cryptocurrency Essentials: Key Concepts and Terminology

The world of cryptocurrency comes with its own unique vocabulary and concepts that can seem like a foreign language to newcomers. Just as learning any new skill requires mastering the basics first, understanding cryptocurrency begins with familiarizing yourself with its fundamental building blocks and terminology. This foundational knowledge will serve as your compass as we explore the intricate world of digital assets and blockchain technology. Just as learning the vocabulary and rules of chess is essential before playing your first game, mastering these crypto fundamentals will prepare you for more advanced concepts and practical applications.

In my years of studying cryptocurrency concepts, I've found that the most successful approach is to break down these complex ideas into digestible pieces. We'll explore each term and concept systematically, building a strong foundation that will serve you well in your crypto journey. From understanding the role of miners in transaction verification to grasping the significance of public and private keys in securing your assets, each piece of knowledge adds to your crypto literacy.

Leah, a high school mathematics teacher, found herself increasingly puzzled by her students' conversations about cryptocurrency during lunch breaks. While she understood traditional banking and investments, the crypto terminology they used felt like an alien language. One day, she decided to tackle this knowledge gap systematically, starting with the basics. She began by learning one new crypto concept each day, creating simple analogies to help her understand. When studying blockchain, she likened it to her class gradebook - a permanent record that everyone could see but only she could modify with her special password (private key). For cryptography, she compared it to the secret codes she used to pass notes in her own high school days, but far more sophisticated. Within weeks, not only could she understand her students' conversations, but she also began incorporating crypto concepts into her math lessons, using real-world examples to teach probability and statistics. Her journey from confusion to comprehension perfectly illustrates how breaking down complex crypto concepts into digestible pieces can transform intimidating terminology into accessible knowledge.

As we progress through this chapter, we'll examine the core components that make cryptocurrency possible. We'll explore the intricate dance between miners, nodes, and validators that keeps the network secure and operational. You'll learn about the critical role of cryptography in ensuring transaction security, privacy, and understand how digital signatures verify ownership and authorize transfers.

The terminology we'll cover isn't just a collection of buzzwords - it's the language of a new financial paradigm. Understanding these terms and concepts will empower you to participate confidently in the crypto ecosystem, whether you're interested in investing, trading, or simply wanting to understand this revolutionary technology better. Each concept builds upon the previous one, creating a comprehensive framework for understanding how cryptocurrency works at a fundamental level.

By the end of this chapter, you'll have developed a solid grasp of the essential vocabulary and concepts that form the foundation of cryptocurrency knowledge. This understanding will serve as your gateway to more advanced topics and practical applications in the chapters that follow. Let's begin our exploration of these fundamental building blocks that make the world of cryptocurrency possible.

Blockchain Architecture: Understanding the Digital Ledger

At the heart of every cryptocurrency lies a revolutionary technology called blockchain - a digital ledger system that records and verifies transactions across a vast network of computers. Think of it as a digital book of records, but unlike traditional ledgers kept by banks or businesses, this book is distributed across thousands of computers worldwide, making it virtually impossible to alter or manipulate.

The architecture of blockchain is built on several fundamental components working in harmony. First, there are the blocks themselves - digital containers that hold batches of verified transactions. Each block contains not only transaction data but also a timestamp and a unique cryptographic signature called a hash that links it to the previous block. This creates an unbreakable chain of information, where changing any single record would require altering every subsequent block - a task that's practically impossible given the distributed nature of the system.

Nodes play a crucial role in maintaining the blockchain's integrity. These are individual computers running specialized software that participate in the network by storing copies of the blockchain, validating new transactions, and sharing information with other nodes. When a new transaction occurs, it must be verified by multiple nodes before being added to a block. This consensus mechanism ensures that only valid transactions are recorded, preventing fraud and maintaining the network's trustworthiness.

The decentralized nature of blockchain architecture represents a fundamental shift from traditional centralized systems. Unlike banks or other financial institutions that maintain their own private ledgers, blockchain's distributed ledger is transparent and accessible to all participants. Every transaction is recorded across multiple copies of the ledger simultaneously, creating an immutable record that can be traced and verified by anyone on the network.

Cryptography serves as the backbone of blockchain security. Each transaction is secured using advanced cryptographic techniques, including public and private keys that work together to create digital signatures. These signatures verify the authenticity of transactions while maintaining user privacy. The cryptographic hash functions that link blocks together ensure that once data is recorded, it cannot be altered without detection, providing an unprecedented level of security and trust.

Consensus mechanisms form another critical component of blockchain architecture. These protocols determine how the network agrees on which transactions are valid and should be added to the chain. Different cryptocurrencies may use various consensus methods, such as Proof of Work or Proof of Stake, but they all serve the same essential purpose: ensuring that all participants in the network agree on the state of the ledger without requiring a central authority.

The immutability of blockchain records represents one of its most powerful features. Once a transaction is verified and added to a block, it becomes a permanent part of the chain. This creates an unalterable history of all transactions, providing transparency and accountability that was previously impossible with traditional record-keeping systems. This characteristic makes blockchain particularly valuable for applications beyond cryptocurrency, including supply chain management and legal contracts.

Understanding blockchain architecture is crucial because it underpins not just cryptocurrencies but an entire ecosystem of decentralized applications. Technology's ability to create trust through transparency, security through cryptography, and consensus through distributed validation has implications far beyond digital currencies. As we continue to explore the cryptocurrency landscape, this foundational knowledge of blockchain architecture will help you better understand both the opportunities and challenges that lie ahead.

Cryptography and Security: The Foundation of Digital Trust

In the digital realm of cryptocurrency, cryptography serves as the bedrock of security and trust. Much like how traditional banks use vaults and security systems to protect physical assets, cryptocurrencies rely on sophisticated cryptographic techniques to secure digital transactions and protect user assets. These mathematical principles create an unbreakable shield around your digital wealth, ensuring that only you can access and transfer your funds.

At its core, cryptocurrency security revolves around two fundamental cryptographic elements: hash functions and key pairs. Hash functions act as digital fingerprints, creating unique identifiers for every piece of information in the blockchain. These mathematical algorithms transform any input data into a fixed-size string of characters, ensuring that no two different inputs can produce the same output. This property makes hash functions essential for maintaining the integrity of the blockchain, as any attempt to alter a transaction would immediately change its hash value, alerting the network to potential tampering.

The concept of public and private keys forms another crucial pillar of cryptocurrency security. Think of your private key as a master password that grants complete control over your digital assets. This secret number must be kept secure at all times, as anyone who obtains it gains full access to your funds. The public key, derived from your private key through complex mathematics, functions like an email address that others can use to send you cryptocurrency. This asymmetric cryptography system enables secure transactions without revealing sensitive information.

Blockchain technology leverages these cryptographic principles to create an immutable record of all transactions. Each block in the chain contains a cryptographic hash of the previous block, forming an unbreakable link that prevents tampering. This structure, combined with the distributed nature of the blockchain, makes it virtually impossible for malicious actors to alter transaction histories or create fraudulent entries.

The security of cryptocurrency networks is further reinforced through mining and consensus mechanisms. In Bitcoin's case, the Proof of Work system requires miners to solve complex cryptographic puzzles, making it prohibitively expensive and computationally difficult for any single entity to gain control of the network. This distributed security model ensures that the network remains resistant to attacks and manipulation.

Cryptographic signatures play a vital role in verifying transaction authenticity. Every transaction must be signed with the sender's private key, creating mathematical proof that only the rightful owner of the funds authorized the transfer. These digital signatures cannot be forged or reused, providing a level of security that surpasses traditional banking systems.

The trustless nature of cryptocurrency operations represents one of its most revolutionary aspects. Through cryptography, users can conduct transactions without relying on intermediaries or central authorities. The mathematical principles underlying these systems create an environment where trust is established through code rather than institutions, enabling faster, more efficient, and more secure financial transactions.

Wallet security builds upon these cryptographic foundations by implementing additional protective measures. Seed phrases, consisting of carefully selected words, can regenerate private keys if needed. Multi-signature authentication requires multiple private keys to authorize transactions, adding an extra layer of security for high-value accounts. Cold storage solutions keep private keys completely offline, protecting them from online threats and potential hackers.

As cryptocurrency technology continues to evolve, new cryptographic innovations emerge to address emerging security challenges. Smart contract platforms implement formal verification and code auditing to ensure the safety of automated transactions. These ongoing developments in cryptographic security help maintain the integrity and trustworthiness of cryptocurrency systems, making them an increasingly reliable alternative to traditional financial infrastructure.

Key Players and Components: From Miners to Wallets

The cryptocurrency ecosystem operates through a complex network of interconnected players and components, each serving a vital role in maintaining the network's functionality and security. At the heart of this system are miners and validators, who act as the guardians of transaction integrity and network security. These participants compete to validate transactions and add new blocks to the blockchain, ensuring the network remains decentralized and trustworthy.

Miners, particularly in Proof of Work systems like Bitcoin, dedicate substantial computational power to solve complex mathematical puzzles. This process, known as mining, serves two crucial purposes: it validates new transactions and creates new coins. The computational effort required makes it economically unfeasible for any single entity to manipulate the system, thereby maintaining the network's security and integrity.

Validators, on the other hand, operate in Proof of Stake systems by holding and "staking" a certain amount of cryptocurrency as collateral. This approach provides a more energy-efficient alternative to mining while maintaining network security through economic incentives. Validators are chosen to create new blocks based on the size of their stake and their historical performance in maintaining network rules.

Nodes form another crucial component of the cryptocurrency ecosystem. These computers maintain copies of the blockchain and verify transactions, creating a distributed network that ensures no single point of failure exists. Full nodes store complete copies of the blockchain, while lightweight nodes maintain only essential data needed for verification purposes.

Wallets represent the user-facing component of the cryptocurrency system, serving as interfaces for managing digital assets. Despite their name, wallets don't actually store cryptocurrencies - instead, they secure the cryptographic keys needed to access and control funds on the blockchain. These tools come in various forms, from "hot" wallets connected to the internet for convenient transactions to "cold" wallets stored offline for maximum security.

Smart contracts add another layer of functionality to the cryptocurrency ecosystem. These self-executing programs automatically enforce agreement terms written directly into code, enabling a wide range of decentralized applications. From lending platforms to decentralized exchanges, smart contracts have become fundamental building blocks of the modern cryptocurrency landscape.

Stablecoins play a unique role in the ecosystem by providing price stability in an otherwise volatile market. These cryptocurrencies, typically pegged to stable assets like the US dollar, facilitate trading, provide liquidity, and enable easier movement between different cryptocurrencies and traditional financial systems.

Decentralized Applications (dApps) serve as the bridge between users and blockchain protocols, offering intuitive interfaces for accessing various cryptocurrency services. These applications leverage smart contracts to provide traditional financial services in a decentralized manner, eliminating the need for intermediaries while enhancing transparency and reducing costs.

The interaction between these components creates a robust and secure ecosystem for digital transactions. Miners and validators ensure network security, nodes maintain decentralization, wallets provide user access, and smart contracts enable automated execution of agreements. Together, these elements form the foundation of a revolutionary financial system that continues to evolve and expand in capability and reach. As we conclude our exploration of cryptocurrency essentials, it's worth reflecting on the journey we've taken through the fundamental concepts and terminology that form the backbone of this revolutionary technology. Just as Leah's story demonstrated, what initially seems like an intimidating array of technical terms can be transformed into accessible knowledge through systematic learning and practical application.

The core components we've covered – from blockchain architecture to cryptographic security and key network players – work together in a harmonious dance that powers the entire cryptocurrency ecosystem. Understanding these fundamentals isn't just about learning new vocabulary; it's about grasping the building blocks that enable a new form of digital value exchange.

Through our examination of blockchain architecture, we've seen how distributed ledger technology creates an immutable record of transactions, secured by advanced cryptography and maintained by a network of participants. The cryptographic principles we've explored reveal how mathematical innovations provide the foundation of trust in a trustless system, enabling secure transactions without traditional intermediaries.

Our discussion of key players and components has illuminated the roles of miners, validators, nodes, and other crucial participants in maintaining network security and functionality. These various elements, working in concert, create a robust and resilient system that continues to evolve and improve.

As you move forward in your cryptocurrency journey, remember that this foundation of knowledge will serve as your compass, helping you navigate more complex concepts and applications. The terminology and concepts we've covered aren't just theoretical – they're practical tools that will help you make informed decisions about cryptocurrency investment, trading, and usage.

Perhaps most importantly, we've seen how breaking down complex ideas into digestible pieces can transform seemingly impenetrable concepts into clear, actionable knowledge. This approach – methodical learning combined with practical application – will continue to serve you well as you delve deeper into the world of cryptocurrency.

As we prepare to move forward to more advanced topics in the coming chapters, keep in mind that every expert in this field once started where you are now – learning the basics, one concept at a time. Your growing understanding of these fundamental principles puts you on the path to becoming a knowledgeable and confident participant in the cryptocurrency ecosystem.

The journey from confusion to comprehension may seem daunting at first, but as we've seen through our exploration of these essential concepts, each piece of knowledge builds upon the last, creating a solid foundation for understanding this revolutionary technology. Armed with this fundamental understanding, you're now ready to explore more advanced aspects of cryptocurrency in the chapters ahead.

Chapter Four

Digital Wallets: Securing Your Crypto Assets

The security of your cryptocurrency investments begins with understanding how to safely store and protect your digital assets. Just as traditional banks provide vaults and safety deposit boxes for securing physical valuables, the cryptocurrency world offers various types of digital wallets, each with its own unique security features and use cases. Building upon this foundation, we'll explore the several types of digital wallets available and how to choose the right one for your needs. From basic software wallets on your phone to advanced hardware solutions that offer bank-grade security, understanding these options is crucial for anyone stepping into the world of cryptocurrency.

Just as traditional financial systems evolved from keeping money under mattresses to sophisticated bank vaults, cryptocurrency storage has developed multiple layers of security and convenience. Each type of wallet serves a specific purpose in your crypto journey, whether you're an active trader needing quick access to funds or a long-term investor focusing on maximum security.

Consider Arthur's story, a tech-savvy individual who faced a sobering lesson in cryptocurrency wallet management. One evening, while attempting to transfer his newly purchased Bitcoin to a hardware wallet, he accidentally copied the wrong receiving address. His heart nearly stopped as he watched the transaction confirmation appear - his Bitcoin had been sent to an unknown address. This gut-wrenching moment taught him the invaluable lesson of double-checking every detail during cryptocurrency transactions. After hours of research and careful documentation, Arthur developed a comprehensive checklist for wallet security. He now maintains multiple wallet types for different purposes: a hardware wallet for long-term storage, a mobile wallet for everyday transactions, and a properly secured backup of all his recovery phrases. His initial mistake, though costly, led him to develop robust security practices that he now shares with other crypto enthusiasts, emphasizing the importance of understanding wallet security before making any transactions.

In this chapter, we'll break down the essential components of cryptocurrency wallets, from basic terminology to advanced security features. You'll learn how to properly set up and maintain different types of wallets, understand the crucial role of private keys, and implement best practices for securing your digital assets. We'll explore the advantages and limitations of various wallet solutions, helping you make informed decisions about storing your cryptocurrency.

Most importantly, we'll focus on practical, actionable strategies that you can implement immediately to enhance the security of your digital assets. Whether you're just starting with your first cryptocurrency purchase or managing a diverse portfolio, the knowledge gained from this chapter will serve as your foundation for safe and effective digital asset management.

Types of Cryptocurrency Wallets: Hot, Cold, and Hardware Solutions

When it comes to storing your cryptocurrency, you have several distinct options, each offering different balances of security and convenience. Understanding these options is crucial for protecting your digital assets while maintaining the level of access you need for your investment strategy.

Hot wallets represent the most accessible category of cryptocurrency storage. These digital wallets maintain an active connection to the internet, making them ideal for frequent trading or regular transactions. Web wallets, provided by cryptocurrency exchanges, offer convenient access through your browser but store your private keys on external servers. Mobile wallets, installed as smartphone applications, provide on-the-go access to your funds but face risks from device compromise or theft. Desktop wallets, while offering more security through local key storage on your computer, remain vulnerable to malware if proper security measures aren't maintained.

Cold wallets take a fundamentally different approach by staying completely offline, dramatically reducing exposure to online threats. Paper wallets, perhaps the simplest form of cold storage, consist of printed or written private keys and addresses. While immune to cyber-attacks, they're vulnerable to physical damage or loss. More sophisticated cold storage options include dedicated offline computers or USB drives configured for cryptocurrency storage, though these require careful handling to maintain security.

Hardware wallets represent the gold standard in cryptocurrency security, combining the robust protection of cold storage with practical usability. These specialized devices generate and store private keys in a secure offline environment, only connecting briefly to sign transactions when needed. This approach keeps your private keys safe from online threats while still allowing you to manage your cryptocurrency holdings effectively.

The choice between custodial and non-custodial wallets represents another crucial decision in wallet selection. Custodial wallets, typically offered by exchanges, manage private keys on your behalf. While convenient, they put your assets under third-party control, contradicting the fundamental cryptocurrency principle of financial autonomy. Non-custodial wallets, where you maintain full control of your private keys, offer true ownership but require greater responsibility in securing and managing your keys.

For most cryptocurrency investors, a combination of wallet types often proves most effective. You might keep a small amount in a hot wallet for regular transactions while securing the majority of your holdings in a hardware wallet for long-term storage. This hybrid approach balances security with accessibility, allowing you to manage your digital assets efficiently while maintaining strong protection for your main investment.

Regardless of which wallet type you choose, proper security practices remain essential. This includes maintaining secure backups of your recovery phrases, using strong passwords, enabling two-factor authentication where available, and regularly updating your software to protect against emerging threats. Remember that the security of your cryptocurrency ultimately depends not just on the wallet type you choose, but how well you implement and maintain security measures around it.

Security Best Practices and Private Key Management

The security of your cryptocurrency ultimately depends on how well you protect and manage your private keys. Think of a private key as the master password to your digital vault – if someone gains access to it, they have complete control over your cryptocurrency. Unlike traditional banking where you can reset a forgotten password through customer service, lost or stolen private keys often mean permanent loss of your digital assets.

The foundation of private key security begins with proper storage practices. Your private key and seed phrase should never be stored in digital format on internet-connected devices or cloud storage services. Instead, consider writing your seed phrase on durable materials like steel or titanium plates that can withstand fire, water damage, and physical degradation. Store these physical backups in secure locations, potentially using multiple secure locations for redundancy.

Implementing strong password practices forms another crucial layer of security. Every wallet and related account should use unique, complex passwords of at least 16 characters. A reputable password manager can help generate and securely store these complex passwords. Additionally, always enable two-factor authentication (2FA) when available, adding an extra verification step beyond just your password.

For significant cryptocurrency holdings, consider implementing advanced security solutions like multi-signature wallets. These wallets require multiple private keys to authorize transactions, like how a bank vault might require two keys held by different people to open. This approach prevents a single point of failure - even if one key is compromised, your funds remain secure.

Regular security maintenance is equally important. Keep your wallet software and devices updated with the latest security patches. Monitor your accounts for any unauthorized activity and set up alerts where possible. If you suspect any security breach, act quickly to transfer funds to a new, secure wallet.

When managing private keys for business or high-value accounts, consider using hardware security modules (HSMs) or secure enclaves. These specialized hardware solutions provide isolated environments for storing and managing cryptographic keys, offering protection even if the main system is compromised.

Educating yourself about common security threats is vital. Cryptocurrency scams often target private key theft through phishing attempts or malware. Never share your private keys or seed phrases with anyone and be extremely cautious of any service or individual requesting this information. Remember that legitimate cryptocurrency services will never ask for your private keys.

Consider implementing a clear recovery plan in case of emergency. Document your security setup and recovery procedures, then store this information securely where trusted family members or executors can access it if needed. This preparation ensures your digital assets remain accessible to your intended beneficiaries even in worst-case scenarios.

The cryptocurrency space continues to evolve, bringing new security challenges and solutions. Stay informed about emerging best practices and be prepared to adapt your security measures accordingly. Remember that the strongest security systems can be undermined by poor operational practices - maintaining consistent security habits is just as important as having robust technical protections in place.

Backup Strategies and Recovery Methods

Creating comprehensive backup strategies for your cryptocurrency wallet is as crucial as the initial security measures themselves. Just as you wouldn't keep all your traditional wealth in a single location without backup documentation, your digital assets require thoughtful redundancy and recovery planning to ensure their safety and accessibility.

The foundation of any crypto backup strategy starts with proper seed phrase management. Your seed phrase, typically a series of 12 or 24 words, serves as the master key to recover your entire wallet. Consider creating multiple copies of this vital information using different storage methods. A common approach involves writing the seed phrase on durable materials like steel or titanium plates that can withstand fire, water damage, and physical degradation. These physical backups should be stored in secure, separate locations to protect against localized disasters or theft.

Digital backups require careful consideration and implementation. While storing wallet information in cloud services might seem convenient, it introduces significant risks of potential breaches or unauthorized access. If you choose to create digital backups, always use strong encryption and consider splitting the information across multiple secure locations. Some advanced users implement what's known as Shamir's Secret Sharing, a cryptographic technique that divides backup information into multiple parts, requiring a specific number of pieces to reconstruct the whole.

Redundancy plays a vital role in effective backup strategies. The 3-2-1 backup rule, adapted for cryptocurrency storage, suggests maintaining at least three copies of your critical wallet information, stored on two different types of media, with one copy kept at an off-site location. This approach provides multiple layers of protection against various forms of loss or damage.

When it comes to recovery methods, preparation and testing are essential. Regularly verify that your backup information is complete and accurate by performing test recoveries on small amounts. This practice helps ensure your backup strategy works as intended while familiarizing you with the recovery process before you need it in an emergency.

Social recovery systems represent an emerging solution for backup and recovery. These systems allow you to designate trusted individuals or "guardians" who can collectively help restore access to your wallet if needed. While this approach adds complexity, it provides an additional layer of security and can be particularly valuable for estate planning or business continuity.

Emergency response planning should be an integral part of your backup strategy. Document clear procedures for what actions to take in various scenarios - whether it's a lost device, compromised credentials, or physical damage to backup materials. Include contact information for relevant support services and maintain an updated list of any exchanges or services where your wallet is registered.

As the cryptocurrency ecosystem evolves, new backup and recovery solutions continue to emerge. Hardware wallet manufacturers now offer sophisticated backup features, including encrypted microSD card backups and integration with secure cloud services[44][45]. These innovations provide additional options for creating robust backup strategies while maintaining security.

Regardless of which backup methods you choose, regular review and updates are crucial. Set a schedule to verify your backups, update any stored information, and assess whether your current strategy still meets your needs. The cryptocurrency space moves quickly, and your backup approach should evolve alongside it to incorporate new security best practices and technologies as they emerge.

As we conclude our exploration of digital wallets and cryptocurrency security, it's essential to remember that the safety of your digital assets ultimately depends on the careful implementation of multiple security layers. Throughout this chapter, we've examined various wallet types, security protocols, and backup strategies that form the foundation of responsible cryptocurrency management.

Arthur's story serves as a powerful reminder that even seemingly small oversights in wallet management can have significant consequences. His journey from a costly mistake to developing robust security practices mirrors the learning curve many cryptocurrency users experience. However, by implementing the security measures and backup strategies we've discussed, you can avoid similar pitfalls and protect your digital investments effectively.

The evolving landscape of cryptocurrency storage solutions continues to offer new options for balancing security with accessibility. Whether you choose to combine multiple wallet types for different purposes or focus on maximum security through hardware wallets, the key lies in understanding and implementing appropriate security measures for your specific needs. Remember that proper wallet management isn't just about choosing the right storage solution - it's about maintaining consistent security practices and staying informed about emerging threats and protections.

As you move forward in your cryptocurrency journey, consider regularly reviewing and updating your wallet security strategy. Technology evolves rapidly, and new security challenges emerge constantly. Stay proactive in your approach to protecting your digital assets and never compromise on fundamental security practices like proper key management and backup procedures.

Your cryptocurrency wallet serves as the gateway to your digital assets, making its security paramount to your success in the crypto space. By applying the principles and practices outlined in this chapter, you're well-equipped to protect your investments while maintaining the flexibility needed to participate in the digital economy effectively. Remember, in the world of cryptocurrency, you are your own bank - and with that power comes the responsibility to implement and maintain robust security measures.

Chapter Five

Smart Trading: Navigation of Cryptocurrency Exchanges

The world of cryptocurrency exchanges can seem like navigating through a complex maze of numbers, charts, and unfamiliar terms. Yet, understanding how to effectively use these digital marketplaces is crucial for anyone serious about participating in the cryptocurrency ecosystem. The transition from traditional financial markets to cryptocurrency exchanges marks a significant evolution in how we trade and exchange value. While the underlying principles of trading remain similar, the unique characteristics of digital assets and blockchain technology introduce new considerations and responsibilities for traders.

Navigating cryptocurrency exchanges requires a blend of technical understanding, security awareness, and strategic thinking. Unlike traditional stock exchanges that operate during set business hours, crypto markets never sleep – they operate 24/7, creating both opportunities and challenges for investors. This constant activity means that proper exchange selection, security protocols, and trading strategies become even more crucial for success.

Understanding different types of cryptocurrency exchanges – from centralized platforms to decentralized protocols – forms the foundation of effective trading. Each type offers distinct advantages and considerations in terms of liquidity, security, and available trading pairs. Whether you're planning to make your first crypto purchase or looking to actively trade across multiple platforms, knowing how to evaluate and use these exchanges safely is essential.

During my early days of trading, I encountered Micah, a real estate investor who had lost access to his exchange account after failing to enable two-factor authentication. He had accumulated a significant portfolio but hadn't taken the necessary security precautions. Micah's experience taught him the hard way about the importance of security measures in cryptocurrency trading. After regaining access to his account through a lengthy verification process, he became an advocate for exchange security best practices. He implemented multiple authentication factors, used hardware security keys, and regularly updated his security settings. Micah's story serves as a powerful reminder that in the world of cryptocurrency trading, security should never be an afterthought – it must be the foundation upon which all trading activities are built. Today, he helps other traders understand that successful trading isn't just about making profitable trades; it's about protecting your assets through proper security protocols and exchange best practices.

As we explore the intricacies of cryptocurrency exchanges in this chapter, we'll focus on practical knowledge that helps you navigate these digital marketplaces safely and effectively. From understanding different order types to implementing security measures, you'll learn the essential skills needed to participate in the cryptocurrency market with confidence. Remember, successful trading isn't just about timing the market – it's about building a strong foundation of knowledge and best practices that protect your investments while maximizing your potential for success.

Understanding Exchange Types and Features

Cryptocurrency exchanges come in several distinct varieties, each offering unique features and benefits for different types of traders. Understanding these differences is crucial for making informed decisions about where to trade and store your digital assets. The most common type is the centralized exchange (CEX), which operates similarly to traditional stock exchanges. These platforms act as trusted intermediaries, holding user funds and facilitating trades through an order book system that matches buyers with sellers.

Centralized exchanges like Binance, Coinbase, and Kraken offer robust security features, including regular audits, insurance coverage, and secure storage solutions for private keys. They typically require identity verification to comply with regulatory requirements, which can provide an additional layer of protection for users. While this may reduce anonymity, it offers easier resolution of account issues through established customer service channels and protection against fraud through registered business operations.

On the other side of the spectrum are decentralized exchanges (DEXs), which represent a fundamental shift in how cryptocurrency trading can occur. These platforms enable direct peer-to-peer trading through smart contracts, eliminating the need for traditional intermediaries. Popular DEXs like Uniswap and PancakeSwap use automated market makers (AMMs) to determine prices and provide liquidity through pooled user funds. While DEXs offer enhanced privacy and control over assets, they may present different security challenges and often require more technical knowledge to use effectively.

Hybrid exchanges attempt to bridge the gap between centralized and decentralized models, offering enhanced security while maintaining improved usability. These platforms aim to combine the best features of both worlds, though they're still evolving and relatively new to the ecosystem. Additionally, specialized derivative trading platforms focus on more complex financial instruments like futures contracts, catering to sophisticated traders who employ advanced strategies.

When selecting an exchange, several key features deserve careful consideration. The trading mechanism - whether traditional order books or automated market makers - affects how trades are executed and prices are determined. Security measures, including two-factor authentication, cold storage of assets, and regular security audits, should be thoroughly evaluated. Regulatory compliance and geographical restrictions can impact access to certain features or the platform itself.

Liquidity is another crucial factor, as it affects your ability to execute trades at desired prices without significant slippage. Major centralized exchanges typically offer deeper liquidity pools, especially for popular trading pairs. However, some decentralized exchanges have developed innovative solutions to address liquidity challenges through protocol-level incentives and yield farming programs.

Fee structures vary significantly across different exchange types. Centralized exchanges often charge trading fees, withdrawal fees, and sometimes deposit fees. Decentralized exchanges may have lower trading fees but require users to pay blockchain network fees (gas fees) for each transaction. Understanding these cost structures is essential for developing effective trading strategies and managing overall expenses.

The user interface and available trading tools can significantly impact your trading experience. Centralized exchanges typically offer more sophisticated trading interfaces with advanced charting tools, multiple order types, and detailed market analysis features. While decentralized exchanges have made significant strides in improving user experience, they may still require more technical knowledge to navigate effectively.

Regardless of which type of exchange you choose, implementing proper security practices remains paramount. This includes using strong passwords, enabling all available security features, and maintaining careful control over access to your accounts. Remember that different exchanges serve different purposes - what works best for one trader may not be optimal for another, depending on their trading goals, technical expertise, and risk tolerance.

Security Measures and Best Practices for Trading

In the fast-paced world of cryptocurrency trading, implementing robust security measures isn't just a recommendation - it's an absolute necessity. The digital nature of cryptocurrency makes it particularly vulnerable to various forms of cyber threats, from sophisticated hacking attempts to social engineering attacks. Understanding and implementing comprehensive security practices can mean the difference between successful trading and devastating losses.

The foundation of trading security begins with proper authentication methods. Multi-Factor Authentication (MFA) and Two-Factor Authentication (2FA) serve as critical front-line defenses against unauthorized access to trading accounts. While SMS-based 2FA is common, security experts strongly recommend using mobile authentication apps like Google Authenticator instead, as these provide superior protection against SIM-swapping attacks and other common vulnerabilities.

When selecting a cryptocurrency exchange, security infrastructure should be a primary consideration. Leading exchanges implement multiple layers of protection, including advanced encryption standards, regular security audits, and sophisticated monitoring systems. The most secure platforms maintain the majority of user funds in cold storage - offline wallets physically isolated from internet-connected systems - while keeping only a small percentage in hot wallets for immediate trading needs.

Personal security practices play an equally crucial role in protecting your trading activities. Creating strong, unique passwords for each platform you use is essential, as password reuse across multiple services can create significant vulnerabilities. Additionally, maintaining separate email addresses for trading accounts and enabling all available security features can help create multiple layers of protection against potential threats.

Phishing attacks represent one of the most common threats to cryptocurrency traders. These sophisticated scams often involve fake websites or emails that perfectly mimic legitimate exchanges. To protect against such attacks, always verify website URLs carefully, bookmark official exchange websites, and never click on links in unsolicited emails claiming to be from your exchange. Remember that legitimate exchanges will never ask for your private keys or security credentials via email or messaging platforms.

Regular monitoring of account activity is another crucial security practice. Many exchanges offer notification systems for login attempts, withdrawals, and other significant account actions. Enabling these alerts can help you quickly identify and respond to any unauthorized access attempts. Additionally, reviewing your trading history and account balance regularly can help you spot any suspicious activities early.

When it comes to storing cryptocurrency, the old adage "don't keep all your eggs in one basket" applies perfectly. While keeping some funds on exchanges is necessary for active trading, storing significant holdings in personal hardware wallets provides an additional layer of security. These physical devices store your private keys offline, protecting them from online threats while giving you complete control over your assets.

IP address and device management also plays a crucial role in maintaining account security. Many exchanges now offer features to whitelist specific IP addresses or devices for account access. This means that even if an attacker obtains your login credentials, they won't be able to access your account from an unauthorized device or location. Similarly, using a Virtual Private Network (VPN) while trading can help protect your connection from potential eavesdropping or man-in-the-middle attacks.

Maintaining detailed records of your trading activities isn't just important for tax purposes - it's also a crucial security measure. Regular backups of your trading history, transaction records, and account details can prove invaluable if you need to verify past activities or resolve potential disputes. These records should be stored securely, preferably in encrypted format, and backed up in multiple locations.

Finally, staying informed about the latest security threats and best practices is essential in the ever-evolving cryptocurrency landscape. Security measures that were adequate yesterday might not be sufficient tomorrow, making continuous education and adaptation crucial for maintaining robust protection of your digital assets. Remember that security in cryptocurrency trading isn't a one-time setup - it's an ongoing process that requires regular attention and updates to remain effective.

Basic Trading Strategies and Order Types

Trading in cryptocurrency markets requires understanding both basic strategies and the various order types available for executing trades. While the crypto market operates 24/7 and can be highly volatile, having a solid grasp of fundamental trading approaches and tools can help investors navigate these digital waters more effectively.

One of the most beginner-friendly strategies is Dollar-Cost Averaging (DCA), where investors purchase a fixed amount of cryptocurrency at regular intervals regardless of the current market price. This methodical approach helps reduce the impact of market volatility while removing the pressure of trying to time the market perfectly. DCA has proven particularly valuable for those seeking a hands-off, long-term approach to crypto investing.

For those interested in more active trading, swing trading offers a middle ground between day trading and long-term investing. Swing traders typically hold positions for days or weeks to capture medium-term price movements. This strategy requires less constant attention than day trading while still allowing traders to capitalize on market trends and reversals. Successful swing traders often combine fundamental analysis of projects with technical indicators to identify potential entry and exit points.

Trend trading represents another popular strategy, focusing on identifying and following longer-term market movements. Traders using this approach buy during established uptrends and sell during downtrends, often using moving averages or momentum indicators to confirm their decisions. While this strategy requires patience and discipline, it can help traders avoid the stress of short-term market fluctuations.

Understanding order types is equally crucial for executing these strategies effectively. Market orders execute immediately at the current market price, making them ideal for situations requiring quick entry or exit. However, they may result in slippage - getting filled at a different price than expected - especially during volatile periods.

Limit orders provide more control by allowing traders to specify the exact price at which they want to buy or sell. These orders only execute when the market reaches the specified price, making them valuable tools for implementing predetermined trading strategies. For example, a trader might set a limit buy order below the current market price, hoping to catch a temporary dip.

Risk management remains paramount in cryptocurrency trading and stop-loss orders serve as a crucial tool in this regard. These orders automatically sell a position when the price drops to a predetermined level, helping protect against significant losses. Similarly, take-profit orders allow traders to lock in gains by automatically selling when a specific profit target is reached.

The stop-limit order combines elements of both stop-loss and limit orders, offering more precise control over trade execution. When the market reaches the stop price, it triggers a limit order rather than an immediate market order. This can help prevent unexpected execution prices during highly volatile periods.

Regardless of which strategy or order types you employ, successful trading requires disciplined risk management. Industry experts consistently emphasize the importance of never risking more than a small percentage of your portfolio on any single trade - typically 1-2%. This approach helps ensure that no single trade can significantly impact on your overall trading capital.

For beginners, starting with simpler strategies like DCA or basic trend following often proves most effective. These approaches allow new traders to gain experience with market dynamics while minimizing potential losses from complex trading techniques. As traders develop their skills and understanding, they can gradually incorporate more sophisticated strategies and order types into their trading arsenal.

Remember that technical analysis tools can help confirm entry and exit points, but they should always be used in conjunction with proper risk management techniques. Successful traders typically combine multiple indicators and time frames to build a more complete picture of market conditions before making trading decisions.

As we conclude our exploration of cryptocurrency exchanges and trading, it's essential to reflect on the core principles that will guide your journey in digital asset trading. Throughout this chapter, we've covered the foundational elements of exchange selection, security protocols, and trading strategies that form the backbone of successful cryptocurrency trading.

The story of Micah's close call with account security serves as a powerful reminder that in the cryptocurrency world, knowledge and preparation are your strongest assets. His experience underscores a crucial lesson: trading success isn't merely about making profitable trades—it's about building a comprehensive approach that prioritizes security, employs sound strategy, and maintains disciplined risk management.

Navigating cryptocurrency exchanges requires a delicate balance of technical understanding and practical application. We've explored various exchange types, from centralized platforms with their robust security features to decentralized exchanges offering greater autonomy. Each comes with its own set of advantages and considerations, emphasizing that there's no one-size-fits-all solution in cryptocurrency trading.

The security measures we've discussed—from two-factor authentication to IP whitelisting—form an essential shield protecting your digital assets. Remember that security in cryptocurrency trading isn't a static setup but an ongoing process requiring regular updates and vigilance. As the crypto landscape continues to evolve, staying informed about the latest security threats and best practices remains crucial.

We've examined various trading strategies and order types, from the beginner-friendly dollar-cost averaging to more sophisticated approaches like swing trading. These tools and strategies provide a framework for making informed trading decisions while managing risk effectively. The key is finding an approach that aligns with your goals, risk tolerance, and available time commitment.

As you move forward in your cryptocurrency trading journey, remember that success often comes not from complex strategies or perfect market timing, but from consistent application of fundamental principles. Start with basic approaches, focus on security, and gradually expand your trading toolkit as you gain experience and confidence.

In the next chapter, we'll explore risk management strategies in greater detail, building upon the foundation we've established here. The skills and knowledge you've gained about exchanges and trading will serve as crucial building blocks for developing a comprehensive approach to protecting and growing your cryptocurrency investments.

Your journey in cryptocurrency trading is unique, and the path to success lies in adapting these principles to your individual circumstances while maintaining unwavering commitment to security and risk management. Remember, in the dynamic world of cryptocurrency trading, patience, discipline, and continuous learning are your most valuable assets.

Chapter Six

Risk Management: Protecting Your Digital Investments

The world of cryptocurrency investing can feel like navigating through a digital minefield, where one wrong step could lead to significant losses. Understanding and implementing proper risk management strategies isn't just recommended—it's absolutely essential for long-term success in the crypto space. Just as traditional investors carefully manage their portfolio risks through diversification and hedging strategies, cryptocurrency investors must develop robust risk management practices tailored to digital assets. The volatile nature of cryptocurrency markets, combined with their 24/7 trading cycles and unique security challenges, demands a comprehensive approach to protecting your investments.

In this chapter, we'll explore essential strategies for safeguarding your digital assets, from basic security protocols to advanced risk management techniques. We'll examine how to create and implement effective security measures, develop contingency plans, and maintain a balanced approach to risk in your crypto portfolio.

During a community cryptocurrency workshop I was co-hosting, I met Annabel, a retired teacher who had lost access to her crypto wallet after misplacing her recovery phrase. She had written it down on what she thought was a secure piece of paper, only to accidentally discard it during spring cleaning. Her story became a powerful lesson for everyone in the room about the importance of proper security measures. Together, we worked through creating a comprehensive backup system for her new wallet, implementing a multi-signature setup, and establishing a secure recovery phrase storage protocol. Annabel's experience taught us all that even the most basic security oversights can have serious consequences. Today, she helps other seniors in her community understand the importance of proper cryptocurrency security practices, turning her near-disaster into a valuable teaching opportunity. Her story perfectly illustrates why having robust security measures and risk management strategies isn't just about protecting assets—it's about ensuring peace of mind in your crypto journey.

As we delve deeper into risk management strategies, remember that successful crypto investing isn't just about choosing the right assets—it's about protecting what you've built. Whether you're dealing with market volatility, security threats, or operational risks, having a well-thought-out risk management framework is crucial for long-term success in the cryptocurrency space.

Through practical examples and step-by-step guidance, this chapter will equip you with the knowledge and tools needed to develop your own risk management strategy. From understanding different types of risks to implementing specific protection measures, you'll learn how to navigate the crypto landscape while keeping your investments secure.

Security Best Practices and Wallet Management

Securing your cryptocurrency investments requires a comprehensive understanding of wallet management and security protocols. Just as you wouldn't leave your life savings in an unlocked drawer, protecting your digital assets demands careful attention to security best practices and proper wallet management techniques.

The foundation of cryptocurrency security begins with understanding the different types of wallets available. Hot wallets, which remain connected to the internet, offer convenience for frequent trading but come with inherent risks due to their online nature. These include mobile applications, desktop software, and exchange-based wallets. Cold storage solutions, like hardware wallets and paper wallets, provide enhanced security by keeping your private keys offline and away from potential cyber threats.

Implementing strong security measures starts with proper private key management. Your private key represents absolute ownership of your cryptocurrency – if someone gains access to it, they can control your assets. Never share your private keys or recovery phrases with anyone, and store backup copies in multiple secure, geographically distributed locations. For significant holdings, consider implementing multi-signature solutions that require multiple approvals for transactions.

Authentication security forms another crucial layer of protection. Use unique, complex passwords for each cryptocurrency service and implement hardware-based two-factor authentication whenever possible. Avoid SMS-based verification due to vulnerabilities to SIM swapping attacks. For high-value cryptocurrency management, consider using dedicated devices that aren't used for general internet browsing or other activities.

Safe transaction practices can help prevent costly mistakes. Always verify recipient addresses multiple times before sending any cryptocurrency. Start with small test transactions before making large transfers and utilize address whitelisting features when available. Be extremely wary of unexpected "giveaways" or investment opportunities, as these often mask malicious intentions.

A multi-layered security approach provides the most robust protection for your digital assets. This includes implementing a tiered wallet strategy, where you maintain separate wallets for daily transactions and long-term storage. Regular monitoring of wallet addresses and transaction histories helps identify any unauthorized activity early. Keep all software, firmware, and applications updated to protect against known vulnerabilities.

Developing a comprehensive backup strategy is essential for protecting against both technical failures and human error. Create redundant copies of recovery phrases, consider encryption for digital backups, and regularly test your recovery procedures. Document access methods for trusted individuals in case of emergency, ensuring your digital assets remain accessible to intended heirs.

Balancing security with usability remains a crucial consideration. While maximum security might suggest keeping all assets in cold storage, practical usage often requires maintaining some funds in more accessible hot wallets. The key is finding the right balance for your specific needs while maintaining strong security practices across all storage solutions.

Regular security audits help ensure your protection measures remain effective. Review your security protocols periodically, stay informed about emerging threats, and adapt your strategies as new security solutions become available. Remember that cryptocurrency security is not a one-time setup but an ongoing process requiring vigilance and adaptation. The monitoring of crypto-assets and their risks requires a clear understanding of the crypto-asset ecosystem and the potential channels through which risks could spread to the financial system and the broader economy.

Portfolio Diversification and Risk Assessment

In the dynamic world of cryptocurrency, portfolio diversification stands as a crucial strategy for managing risk while maintaining potential for returns. Just as traditional investors spread their investments across different asset classes, cryptocurrency investors must thoughtfully distribute their holdings across various digital assets and sectors to build resilience against market volatility.

A well-structured cryptocurrency portfolio typically follows a balanced allocation framework. While specific percentages should align with individual risk tolerance and goals, many experienced investors maintain substantial positions in established cryptocurrencies like Bitcoin and Ethereum as foundational holdings. These major cryptocurrencies often provide relative stability compared to smaller altcoins and represent core blockchain technology adoption.

Diversification in the cryptocurrency space extends beyond simply owning multiple digital currencies. Effective diversification requires strategic exposure across different sectors within the crypto ecosystem. This includes allocating investments across privacy coins, decentralized finance (DeFi) platforms, utility tokens, and other emerging categories. Each sector presents unique value propositions and risk profiles, helping to create a more balanced portfolio.

When assessing risk in cryptocurrency investments, both systematic and asset-specific factors must be carefully evaluated. Systematic risks affect the entire cryptocurrency market and include regulatory changes, shifts in market sentiment, technological developments, and broader macroeconomic conditions. These factors can cause market-wide movements and must be considered when determining overall portfolio exposure.

Asset-specific risks require detailed analysis of individual cryptocurrencies. This includes examining technical risks like potential code vulnerabilities, team risks such as developer expertise and project leadership, adoption challenges, and tokenomics including distribution patterns and economic incentives. Understanding these specific risk factors helps inform appropriate position sizing and risk management strategies.

Ongoing portfolio management plays a vital role in maintaining effective diversification. As market conditions change and asset values fluctuate, portfolio allocations naturally drift from their target percentages. Implementing regular rebalancing helps maintain desired risk exposure while potentially capitalizing on market movements. This might involve taking profits from high-performing assets and reallocating to maintain balanced exposure.

Research from financial institutions has demonstrated that cryptocurrencies can potentially enhance portfolio efficiency when combined thoughtfully with other assets. However, the high volatility and evolving nature of crypto markets make it essential to maintain appropriate position sizes and regularly reassess risk tolerance.

Beyond direct cryptocurrency holdings, investors may consider alternative approaches to enhance portfolio diversification. This could include exposure to blockchain technology companies, cryptocurrency mining operations, or investments across multiple blockchain ecosystems. These alternatives can provide additional layers of diversification while maintaining exposure to the growth potential of the digital asset industry.

Due diligence remains crucial before adding any cryptocurrency to a portfolio. This includes thorough examination of the underlying technology, evaluation of the development team, review of project documentation, and assessment of community support and engagement. Regular monitoring of these factors helps ensure portfolio allocations continue to align with investment objectives and risk tolerance.

While the cryptocurrency market offers significant opportunities, its inherent volatility makes diversification not just a strategy but a necessity. By thoughtfully spreading investments across different digital assets, sectors, and investment approaches while maintaining appropriate risk management practices, investors can build more resilient portfolios designed to weather market fluctuations while maintaining exposure to the growth potential of digital assets.

Emergency Response Planning and Recovery Strategies

In the fast-moving world of cryptocurrency, having a well-structured emergency response plan isn't just prudent—it's essential for survival. The digital nature of cryptocurrency assets, combined with their irreversible transaction characteristics, makes them particularly vulnerable to various threats that require immediate and decisive action when incidents occur.

A comprehensive emergency response plan begins with identifying potential threats and vulnerabilities. These can range from technical failures and security breaches to market-related emergencies and regulatory changes. Each type of emergency requires specific response protocols and having these documented and readily accessible can mean the difference between quick recovery and catastrophic loss.

The foundation of any emergency response strategy starts with secure backup systems. This includes maintaining encrypted copies of private keys, seed phrases, and wallet recovery information in multiple secure locations. Consider using both digital and physical storage methods, ensuring they're geographically distributed to protect against localized disasters. However, never store this sensitive information on internet-connected devices or cloud services without proper encryption.

Implementing a tiered response system helps prioritize actions during emergencies. The first tier focuses on immediate containment—actions taken within the first minutes or hours of discovering an incident. This might include freezing accounts, disconnecting compromised devices from networks, or initiating emergency transfers to secure wallets. The second tier involves assessment and documentation, while the third tier encompasses long-term recovery and prevention of future incidents.

Real-time monitoring and alert systems play a crucial role in emergency response effectiveness. Setting up automated notifications for unusual transaction patterns, significant price movements, or suspicious login attempts can provide early warning of potential problems. The sooner an incident is detected, the better the chances of successful containment and recovery.

When establishing recovery protocols, consider both technical and operational aspects. Technical recovery might involve restoring wallets from secure backups or initiating multi-signature recovery procedures. Operational recovery focuses on maintaining business continuity, managing stakeholder communications, and implementing lessons learned to prevent future incidents.

Documentation becomes particularly critical during emergencies. Maintain detailed logs of all response actions, including timestamps, personnel involved, and outcomes. This information proves invaluable for post-incident analysis and may be required for insurance claims or legal proceedings. Keep templates ready for different types of incident reports and stakeholder communications.

Regular testing of emergency procedures helps ensure their effectiveness when needed. Conduct periodic drills simulating different types of emergencies, from simple wallet recovery exercises to full-scale incident response scenarios. These tests help identify gaps in procedures and ensure team members understand their roles during actual emergencies.

Establishing relationships with key service providers and legal counsel before emergencies occur can expedite response times when incidents happen. Keep updated contact information for exchanges, wallet providers, and cybersecurity experts readily available. Consider retaining legal counsel familiar with cryptocurrency-related incidents, as their expertise can be crucial during recovery efforts.

Finally, maintain a continuous improvement cycle for emergency response planning. After any incident or drill, conduct thorough reviews to identify areas for improvement. Stay informed about new threats and security measures in the cryptocurrency space and update response plans accordingly. Remember that emergency response planning is not a one-time effort but an ongoing process that evolves with the changing landscape of digital assets.

By implementing these comprehensive emergency response and recovery strategies, cryptocurrency investors can better protect their assets and respond effectively when incidents occur. While no plan can prevent all emergencies, having well-thought-out response protocols significantly improves the chances of successful recovery and minimizes potential losses.

As we conclude this vital chapter on protecting your digital investments, it's crucial to reflect on the fundamental principles we've explored. Risk management in cryptocurrency isn't about following a set of rules—it's about developing a mindset that prioritizes security and strategic thinking in every aspect of your crypto journey.

The story of Annabel, which opened our chapter, serves as a powerful reminder that even the most basic oversight in security can have significant consequences. Yet, her experience also demonstrates how proper education and implementation of security measures can transform potential disasters into valuable learning opportunities. Through examining security best practices, portfolio diversification strategies, and emergency response planning, we've built a comprehensive framework for protecting digital investments.

Key takeaways from this chapter include the critical importance of implementing multi-layered security measures, from proper wallet management to robust authentication protocols. We've learned that diversification extends beyond simply holding multiple cryptocurrencies—it requires thoughtful allocation across different sectors and risk levels within the crypto ecosystem. Perhaps most importantly, we've recognized that emergency response planning isn't an optional extra but a fundamental component of risk management.

Moving forward, remember that risk management in cryptocurrency is not a one-time setup but an ongoing process requiring regular review and adjustment. As the crypto landscape evolves, so should your security measures and risk management strategies too. Stay informed about emerging threats, regularly assess your security protocols, and maintain vigilance in protecting your digital assets.

Through understanding and implementing the strategies we've discussed, you're better equipped to navigate the volatile world of cryptocurrency while protecting your investments. Remember, successful crypto investing isn't only about maximizing returns—it's about building a sustainable, secure foundation for your digital asset journey. As we move into our next chapter on investment strategies, keep these risk management principles in mind. They will serve as the bedrock upon which you can build a robust and resilient cryptocurrency portfolio.

Chapter Seven

Investment Strategies: Building a Balanced Crypto Portfolio

The art of building a balanced cryptocurrency portfolio extends far beyond simply buying popular tokens and hoping for the best. Like a master chef carefully selecting and combining ingredients for a perfect dish, successful crypto investors must thoughtfully choose and proportion their digital assets to create a resilient investment strategy. Just as a master chef carefully refines their recipes through trial and error, successful cryptocurrency investors must develop and refine their portfolio strategies over time. The crypto market's unique characteristics - its volatility, 24/7 trading, and diverse asset classes - demand a thoughtful approach to portfolio construction that goes beyond simple diversification.

Understanding how to build a balanced crypto portfolio requires grasping both fundamental investment principles and the specific nuances of digital assets. While traditional investment wisdom about diversification and risk management still applies, the cryptocurrency market introduces new considerations that must be carefully weighed. From market capitalization and trading volume to technological fundamentals and developmental roadmaps, each factor plays a crucial role in portfolio decisions.

Jamie had always considered herself a cautious investor, sticking mainly to traditional assets until 2019. After months of research, she decided to allocate 5% of her investment portfolio to cryptocurrencies. However, her initial approach was flawed – she invested heavily in a single altcoin that a friend recommended, breaking the fundamental rule of diversification. When the market experienced a significant correction in 2020, Jamie's concentrated position led to substantial losses. This experience taught her a valuable lesson about the importance of portfolio balance. She restructured her crypto holdings, dividing them across established cryptocurrencies, promising DeFi projects, and a small allocation to carefully researched emerging tokens. She also implemented a strict rebalancing schedule and position sizing rules. By 2021, when the market became volatile again, Jamie's diversified approach helped her weather the storm much more effectively, with some assets offsetting losses in others. Her story illustrates how a balanced, well-thought-out portfolio strategy can make the difference between success and failure in cryptocurrency investing.

In this chapter, we'll explore the essential components of building and maintaining a resilient cryptocurrency portfolio. We'll examine proven strategies for asset allocation, risk assessment, and portfolio rebalancing that can help you navigate the dynamic crypto market. Whether you're just starting your investment journey or looking to optimize an existing portfolio, understanding these fundamental principles will help you build a stronger foundation for long-term success in the cryptocurrency space.

Portfolio Diversification Principles and Asset Allocation

Diversification stands as a cornerstone principle in cryptocurrency investment strategy, much like its role in traditional finance. However, the unique characteristics of digital assets require a specialized approach to building a well-balanced portfolio. The crypto market's heightened volatility and 24/7 trading environment make diversification not just important, but essential for managing risk while maintaining exposure to potential growth opportunities.

A well-diversified cryptocurrency portfolio typically begins with a foundation of established assets like Bitcoin and Ethereum, which often serve as the market's benchmark cryptocurrencies. These major assets typically comprise 40-50% of a balanced portfolio, providing relative stability and market correlation. Stablecoins represent another crucial component, offering a hedge against market volatility and maintaining readily available liquidity for opportunistic investments.

Beyond these foundational elements, investors should consider spreading their holdings across different sectors within the cryptocurrency ecosystem. This might include allocations to DeFi (Decentralized Finance) projects, privacy-focused coins, gaming and metaverse tokens, and infrastructure projects. Each sector offers unique value propositions and growth potential, while potentially responding differently to market conditions and external factors.

Investment strategy diversification provides another layer of portfolio resilience. This approach combines long-term holdings with shorter-term tactical positions, while potentially incorporating yield-generating activities like staking or liquidity provision. The specific balance between these strategies should align with individual risk tolerance and investment goals.

When implementing a diversification strategy, it's crucial to maintain regular portfolio monitoring and rebalancing. Market movements can quickly shift target allocations, requiring periodic adjustments to maintain desired exposure levels. This process should include both profit-taking from well-performing assets and reallocation to maintain strategic positioning.

Risk tolerance plays a vital role in determining appropriate allocation percentages. Conservative investors might prefer higher allocations to established cryptocurrencies and stablecoins, while more aggressive investors could increase exposure to emerging projects and alternative assets. Regardless of risk appetite, thorough research remains essential before adding any asset to a portfolio.

The dynamic nature of the cryptocurrency market demands ongoing attention to portfolio composition. Regular assessment of each asset's role in the portfolio, its current market position, and its alignment with investment objectives helps maintain a robust diversification strategy. This includes evaluating factors such as technology fundamentals, team credentials, community support, and tokenomics for each project.

While diversification cannot eliminate all investment risks, it remains one of the most effective tools for managing cryptocurrency portfolio volatility. By spreading investments across various assets, sectors, and strategies, investors can build more resilient portfolios capable of weathering market fluctuations while maintaining exposure to the growth potential of digital assets.

Risk Management and Position Sizing

Risk management in cryptocurrency investing goes beyond simple diversification - it requires a systematic approach to position sizing and capital preservation. The volatile nature of digital assets, where price swings of 10–20% in a single day are common, makes proper risk management essential for long-term success. Understanding and implementing these principles can mean the difference between sustainable growth and devastating losses.

One fundamental approach to risk management is the implementation of strict position sizing rules. The 1–2% rule, borrowed from traditional trading wisdom, suggests risking no more than 1–2% of your total portfolio value on any single position. This ensures that even a series of losing trades won't significantly damage your overall portfolio. For example, if you have a $10,000 portfolio, your maximum risk per position should be $100–200, regardless of how confident you feel about a particular investment.

Stop-loss orders serve as another crucial risk management tool, acting as predetermined exit points to prevent excessive losses. While the highly volatile nature of cryptocurrency markets requires wider stop-loss parameters than traditional assets, setting these limits 10–20% below purchase prices helps maintain portfolio discipline. However, it's important to note that during extreme market conditions, execution of stop-loss orders may not always occur at exactly the specified price.

Dollar-cost averaging (DCA) represents a powerful risk management strategy for long-term cryptocurrency investors. This approach involves investing fixed amounts at regular intervals regardless of market conditions, which helps reduce the impact of volatility and eliminates the stress of trying to time market entries. DCA naturally leads to buying more coins when prices are lower and fewer when prices are higher, potentially improving overall returns while managing risk.

Take-profit levels complement stop-loss orders by locking in gains at predetermined price targets. A common approach involves scaling out of positions gradually - selling portions of holdings as they reach different profit milestones. This strategy allows investors to maintain exposure to potential further upside while securing profits and reducing overall position risk.

Portfolio rebalancing serves as another essential risk management practice. Regular rebalancing, whether monthly or quarterly, helps maintain target asset allocations and prevents any single position from becoming too large relative to the overall portfolio. When one cryptocurrency significantly outperforms others, selling a portion to return to target allocations enforces disciplined profit-taking while managing risk.

The psychological aspect of risk management cannot be overstated in cryptocurrency investing. The extreme volatility can trigger emotional responses that lead to poor decision-making. Successful risk management requires developing the discipline to stick to predetermined strategies regardless of market conditions or emotional impulses. This includes having the patience to wait for proper entry points and the discipline to exit positions when risk parameters are breached.

Advanced investors might consider hedging techniques to manage risk without completely exiting positions. This could involve using options, futures, or inverse ETFs to protect against potential market downturns. However, these sophisticated strategies require thorough understanding and careful implementation to avoid introducing additional risks.

Correlation analysis provides another layer of risk management by helping investors understand how different cryptocurrencies move in relation to each other. Some altcoins closely follow Bitcoin's price movements, while others may have more independent price action. Understanding these relationships helps in building truly diversified portfolios that can better weather market volatility.

Ultimately, successful risk management in cryptocurrency investing requires a comprehensive approach that combines multiple strategies while remaining adaptable to changing market conditions. By implementing proper position sizing, using stop-loss and take-profit orders, practicing regular rebalancing, and maintaining emotional discipline, investors can better protect their capital while participating in the potential growth of digital assets.

Portfolio Rebalancing and Performance Monitoring

Regular portfolio rebalancing and performance monitoring form the cornerstone of successful cryptocurrency investment management. As digital asset markets operate 24/7 with significant volatility, maintaining target allocations requires vigilant oversight and systematic adjustment. This process helps investors stay true to their investment strategy while managing risk in a disciplined manner.

Portfolio rebalancing in cryptocurrency markets typically follows one of three main approaches. Periodic rebalancing involves adjusting allocations at fixed intervals, such as weekly or monthly, regardless of market conditions. Threshold rebalancing triggers adjustments when asset allocations deviate from targets by a predetermined percentage, often 15-20%. A hybrid approach combines both time-based and threshold methods, providing a balanced framework for portfolio maintenance.

Implementing a rebalancing strategy begins with assessing current allocations by converting each asset's value to a base currency and calculating its percentage of the total portfolio. This analysis reveals whether holdings have drifted from their target allocations due to market movements. For example, if Bitcoin was intended to comprise 25% of a portfolio but has appreciated to represent 35%, rebalancing would involve selling some Bitcoin and redistributing the proceeds to underweight assets.

Performance monitoring complements rebalancing by providing crucial insights into portfolio behavior and effectiveness. Modern cryptocurrency investors benefit from various tools and platforms that offer real-time tracking of portfolio metrics, including returns, risk measures, and allocation drift. These technologies enable investors to make data-driven decisions about when and how to rebalance their holdings.

While rebalancing offers significant benefits in risk management and strategy adherence, it's important to consider the associated costs and challenges. Transaction fees can accumulate with frequent trading, potentially eroding returns. Additionally, selling high-performing assets may result in missed opportunities if their upward trajectory continues. Therefore, finding the right balance between maintaining target allocations and minimizing unnecessary transactions becomes crucial.

Research from major crypto portfolio management platforms has demonstrated the value of systematic rebalancing. A notable 2021 study found that investors using threshold rebalancing achieved lower volatility and improved risk-adjusted returns compared to those who maintained static portfolios. This evidence supports the importance of regular portfolio maintenance in cryptocurrency investing.

Automation has emerged as a powerful tool in portfolio rebalancing and monitoring. Many platforms now offer automated rebalancing features that can execute trades based on predetermined rules and thresholds. This technology helps remove emotional bias from the process while ensuring consistent application of investment strategies. However, automated systems should be regularly reviewed and adjusted to ensure they continue to align with investment goals and market conditions.

Successful portfolio management requires a comprehensive approach that combines regular monitoring with disciplined rebalancing. By maintaining target allocations through systematic adjustments, investors can better control risk while participating in the potential growth of digital assets. Whether using manual methods or automated tools, the key lies in consistent application of chosen strategies and regular evaluation of their effectiveness.

As the cryptocurrency market continues to evolve, the importance of robust portfolio management practices becomes increasingly apparent. Regular rebalancing and performance monitoring provide the structure needed to navigate market volatility while maintaining alignment with long-term investment objectives. Through careful attention to these fundamental practices, investors can build more resilient portfolios capable of weathering market fluctuations while pursuing their financial goals. As we conclude this exploration of building a balanced cryptocurrency portfolio, it's worth reflecting on the fundamental principles we've covered and their vital importance in the evolving digital asset landscape. Jamie's journey from a concentrated, high-risk position to a thoughtfully diversified portfolio illustrates the transformative power of applying sound investment principles to cryptocurrency investing.

The key takeaways from this chapter underscore the importance of strategic diversification across different cryptocurrency sectors, systematic risk management through position sizing, and consistent portfolio monitoring and rebalancing. We've seen how successful cryptocurrency investing isn't about chasing the latest trending token or making impulsive decisions based on market hype. Instead, it requires a methodical approach that combines traditional investment wisdom with an understanding of the unique characteristics of digital assets.

Perhaps most importantly, we've learned that building a balanced crypto portfolio is not a one-time event but an ongoing process that requires regular attention and adjustment. The volatile nature of cryptocurrency markets demands vigilance in maintaining target allocations and reassessing investment theses as market conditions evolve. Through proper diversification, risk management, and regular rebalancing, investors can build portfolios capable of weathering market volatility while maintaining exposure to the growth potential of digital assets.

As you move forward in your cryptocurrency investment journey, remember that success comes not from trying to time the market or betting everything on a single promising project, but from building a resilient portfolio that aligns with your risk tolerance and investment goals. Stay committed to your strategy during both market upturns and downturns, and don't let emotions drive your investment decisions.

While the cryptocurrency market continues to mature and evolve, the fundamental principles of portfolio management we've discussed remain constant. By applying these principles consistently and adapting them to changing market conditions, you'll be better positioned to navigate the exciting but challenging world of cryptocurrency investing. Remember, the goal isn't to eliminate all risk – that's impossible in any investment – but to manage it effectively while pursuing your financial objectives in the digital asset space.

Chapter Eight

Security Protocols: Avoiding Scams and Fraud

The cryptocurrency landscape, while revolutionary, has become a breeding ground for sophisticated scams that prey on unsuspecting investors. Understanding the intricate web of security protocols isn't just about protecting your assets—it's about ensuring your peace of mind in an increasingly complex digital financial world. The rise of cryptocurrency has brought with it an unprecedented wave of innovative financial opportunities, but it has also attracted sophisticated criminals who employ increasingly clever tactics to deceive investors. Just as traditional financial markets developed security protocols over time, the crypto space requires vigilance and education to protect assets effectively.

In this chapter, we'll explore common cryptocurrency scams, essential security measures, and proven strategies for safeguarding your digital investments. From phishing attempts to fake ICOs and pump-and-dump schemes, understanding these threats is the first step toward protecting yourself. We'll delve into practical security habits that every crypto investor should develop, including proper wallet management, secure password practices, and the crucial role of two-factor authentication.

Curtis had always considered himself tech-savvy until he received what appeared to be a legitimate email from his cryptocurrency exchange. The message warned about suspicious activity and prompted him to verify his account by clicking a link. Something felt off about the urgency of the request, so he decided to manually check his exchange account through the official website instead. His suspicion proved correct—the email was a sophisticated phishing attempt. By following proper security protocols and trusting his instincts, Curtis avoided what could have been a devastating loss of his entire crypto portfolio. This experience taught him the invaluable lesson that in the crypto world, skepticism and verification are your best allies. He now regularly updates his security measures and helps educate others about the importance of following proper security protocols, knowing that even a moment's lapse in judgment could have costly consequences.

The story highlights a fundamental truth in cryptocurrency security: vigilance and proper protocols aren't just recommendations—they're essential survival tools in the digital asset space. As we explore the various aspects of cryptocurrency security, you'll learn how to develop an eye for suspicious activity and build robust defenses against common threats. Understanding these security measures isn't only about protecting your investments; it's about ensuring you can participate in the cryptocurrency ecosystem with confidence and peace of mind.

Whether you're just starting your crypto journey or you're an experienced investor looking to strengthen your security practices, this chapter will provide you with the knowledge and tools needed to protect your digital assets effectively. We'll examine real-world examples of common scams, explore proven security measures, and discuss emergency response strategies for worst-case scenarios. By the end of this chapter, you'll have a comprehensive understanding of how to identify, prevent, and respond to security threats in the cryptocurrency space.

Common Cryptocurrency Scams and How to Identify Them

The cryptocurrency ecosystem has given rise to numerous sophisticated scams that continue to evolve and adapt.

Understanding these deceptive practices is crucial for protecting your digital assets. One of the most prevalent threats comes in the form of phishing scams, where criminals create convincing replicas of legitimate cryptocurrency exchanges or wallet interfaces. These fraudulent sites often appear nearly identical to their authentic counterparts, making them particularly dangerous for unsuspecting users.

Ponzi and pyramid schemes have also found new life in the crypto space, often disguised as high-yield investment programs or mining operations. These scams promise unrealistic returns and rely on new investor funds to pay earlier participants, creating an unsustainable cycle that inevitably collapses. The decentralized nature of cryptocurrency can make it particularly challenging to recover funds lost to such schemes.

Fake Initial Coin Offerings (ICOs) represent another significant threat to investors. Scammers launch fraudulent fundraising campaigns that mimic legitimate projects, complete with professional-looking websites, whitepapers, and social media presence. Once they've collected sufficient funds, the perpetrators disappear, leaving investors with worthless tokens. This type of scam has become so prevalent that it has led to increased regulatory scrutiny of the entire ICO process.

The "pig butchering" scam has emerged as a particularly insidious threat in recent years. Fraudsters build trust with victims over extended periods through social media or dating apps, gradually introducing them to seemingly legitimate cryptocurrency investment platforms. These sophisticated operations often maintain the illusion of profitability for months before ultimately disappearing with victims' funds.

To protect yourself from these scams, it's essential to recognize common warning signs. Be extremely wary of unsolicited investment opportunities, especially those promising guaranteed returns or using high-pressure sales tactics. Legitimate cryptocurrency projects don't require you to act immediately or share sensitive wallet information. Always verify the authenticity of trading platforms and wallet applications by downloading them from official sources and double-checking website URLs for subtle misspellings or variations.

Man-in-the-middle attacks pose a significant risk, particularly when accessing cryptocurrency accounts through public Wi-Fi networks. These attacks can intercept data transmissions and steal sensitive information, including passwords and private keys. Using secure, private networks and enabling two-factor authentication provides essential protection against such threats.

Malware and hacking attempts continue to target cryptocurrency users through various means. Cybercriminals often deploy malicious software through phishing links or fake applications designed to gain access to crypto wallets or exchange accounts. Maintaining updated security software and being cautious about downloading unknown applications are crucial defensive measures.

Recruitment and job scams have also become increasingly common in the cryptocurrency space. These schemes typically involve fake employment opportunities related to crypto mining, trading, or conversion services. Victims are often required to pay upfront fees or share sensitive information, only to discover the position doesn't exist. Any job offer requiring initial investment should be treated with extreme skepticism.

To effectively protect yourself from cryptocurrency scams, implement a comprehensive security strategy. This includes using reputable exchanges and wallets with strong security protocols, enabling two-factor authentication on all accounts, and conducting thorough research before engaging with any new platform or investment opportunity. Remember that legitimate cryptocurrency projects will never pressure you for immediate action or require you to share private keys or seed phrases.

Essential Security Measures for Protecting Your Digital Assets

Protecting your cryptocurrency investments requires a multi-layered approach to security that goes beyond basic password protection. The cryptocurrency space demands vigilance and adherence to established security protocols to safeguard your digital assets effectively. Understanding and implementing these essential security measures can mean the difference between maintaining control of your investments and falling victim to theft or fraud.

At the foundation of cryptocurrency security lies proper wallet management. The choice between hot wallets (connected to the internet) and cold wallets (offline storage) represents one of the most crucial security decisions investors face. While hot wallets offer convenience for frequent trading, cold storage through hardware wallets provides superior security for long-term holdings. Many experienced investors adopt a hybrid approach, keeping only small amounts in hot wallets for trading while securing the bulk of their assets in cold storage.

Multi-factor authentication (MFA) stands as a critical defense mechanism for all cryptocurrency accounts and wallets. This security layer requires multiple forms of identification, which may include biometric scanning, public key infrastructure, or time-based one-time passwords. Enabling MFA on all crypto-related accounts creates a robust barrier against unauthorized access attempts, even if passwords become compromised.

Network security plays a vital role in protecting digital assets. Conducting cryptocurrency transactions over public Wi-Fi networks exposes investors to significant risks, as even amateur hackers can potentially intercept sensitive information. Using a trusted Virtual Private Network (VPN) creates a secure encrypted digital tunnel that shields your wallet and transaction data from prying eyes. This extra layer of protection becomes especially crucial when accessing cryptocurrency accounts while traveling or using public internet connections.

Proper backup and recovery protocols form another essential component of cryptocurrency security. Regular backups of wallet information, including private keys and recovery phrases, must be stored securely in multiple physical locations. However, these backups themselves require protection through encryption and secure storage methods to prevent unauthorized access. Many investors use fireproof safes or safety deposit boxes to store their backup information, ensuring they can recover their assets even if their primary device fails or becomes compromised.

The Cryptocurrency Security Standards (CCSS) provide a comprehensive framework for securing digital assets. These standards encompass crucial aspects such as key generation, storage procedures, and compromise policies. Following these established guidelines helps investors maintain consistent security practices aligned with industry best practices.

Data protection through encryption serves as another critical security measure. Both data in transit and at rest should be encrypted using robust encryption protocols. This applies not only to wallet information but also to any sensitive data related to your cryptocurrency holdings. Additionally, maintaining up-to-date software and firmware for all cryptocurrency-related applications and hardware devices ensures you're protected against known security vulnerabilities.

Access management represents a crucial aspect of cryptocurrency security. This includes implementing strong password practices and potentially using password managers to securely store and manage credentials. Limiting access to your cryptocurrency accounts and maintaining strict control over user privileges helps prevent unauthorized transactions or account modifications.

Continuous monitoring of accounts and transactions provides an additional security layer. Many exchanges and wallet services offer alert systems that notify users of suspicious activities or unauthorized access attempts. Setting up these notifications and responding promptly to any security alerts can help prevent or minimize potential losses.

Smart contract and token security deserve special attention for investors involved in decentralized finance (DeFi) or other blockchain applications. Understanding the risks associated with smart contracts and ensuring proper testing before engaging with new protocols can help protect against common vulnerabilities in this emerging space.

As the cryptocurrency ecosystem continues to evolve, staying informed about new security threats and best practices becomes increasingly important. Regular security audits of your cryptocurrency holdings and security measures help ensure your protection strategies remain effective against emerging threats. Remember that security in the cryptocurrency space is not a one-time setup but rather an ongoing process requiring regular attention and updates.

Recovery Protocols and Emergency Response Plans

Having strong preventative security measures is essential, but equally important is maintaining clear protocols for responding to potential security breaches or asset loss. A well-structured emergency response plan can mean the difference between recovering compromised assets and permanent loss. Understanding and implementing proper recovery protocols before an incident occurs provides the best chance of successful asset recovery.

The crypto-asset recovery process typically follows four distinct phases: asset tracing, asset freezing and seizing, asset confiscation, and asset realization. Each phase requires specific procedures and documentation to ensure the process remains robust and auditable. Asset tracing involves carefully tracking fund movements across the blockchain, while freezing and seizing requires swift action through appropriate legal channels to prevent further unauthorized transfers.

When developing an emergency response plan, several key components must be included. First, establish clear procedures for reporting and analyzing security incidents, including detailed documentation of all relevant transaction IDs, timestamps, and wallet addresses. Second, implement containment strategies to limit potential damage, such as immediately disconnecting compromised hot wallets from the internet and changing passwords on associated accounts. Third, define specific roles and responsibilities during an emergency, ensuring everyone involved understands their part in the recovery process.

Social recovery systems have emerged as an innovative solution for cryptocurrency asset recovery. These protocols allow users to designate trusted contacts who can assist in wallet recovery through multi-signature approaches. Similarly, threshold schemes require a predetermined number of authorized parties to approve recovery actions, providing an additional layer of security while maintaining the ability to recover assets if access is lost.

Cross-jurisdictional considerations play a crucial role in cryptocurrency recovery efforts, particularly when funds are transferred to service providers in foreign jurisdictions. The process often requires navigating both formal orders and informal cooperation channels through mutual legal assistance protocols. Understanding these jurisdictional requirements beforehand can significantly improve the chances of successful asset recovery.

Professional recovery services have developed systematic approaches to handling cryptocurrency theft or loss. These services typically begin with a comprehensive initial assessment, gathering detailed information about the case and developing customized recovery strategies. They employ specialized tools and blockchain forensics to trace stolen funds while maintaining ongoing communication with affected parties throughout the recovery process.

Redundancy in backup systems forms a critical component of any recovery protocol. Maintaining multiple secure copies of recovery information in different physical locations provides essential protection against various loss scenarios. These backups should be protected through robust encryption tools like AES-256 or Twofish, and consideration should be given to storing critical recovery information on air-gapped computers or specialized hardware solutions.

Prevention remains the best form of protection, but having a comprehensive emergency response plan ensures you're prepared for worst-case scenarios. Regular review and updates to your recovery protocols help ensure they remain effective as the cryptocurrency landscape evolves. Remember that successful asset recovery often depends on how quickly and effectively you can respond to security incidents, making preparation and planning essential components of cryptocurrency security strategy. As we conclude our exploration of cryptocurrency security, it's crucial to recognize that protecting digital assets requires constant vigilance and adaptation. Throughout this chapter, we've examined the multifaceted nature of cryptocurrency security threats and the robust measures needed to safeguard our investments.

From Curtis's close encounter with a sophisticated phishing attempt to our detailed analysis of common scams and essential security protocols, we've seen how proper security measures can mean the difference between success and catastrophe in the crypto space. The cryptocurrency ecosystem continues to evolve, bringing both new opportunities and emerging threats. Understanding and implementing comprehensive security measures isn't just about protecting our investments—it's about contributing to the broader adoption and legitimacy of digital assets. As we've discussed, proper wallet management, strong authentication practices, and clear recovery protocols form the foundation of effective cryptocurrency security.

Perhaps most importantly, we've learned that security in the cryptocurrency space is an ongoing journey rather than a destination. Staying informed about emerging threats, regularly updating security practices, and maintaining proper backup procedures are essential habits for every cryptocurrency investor. The stories and examples shared in this chapter serve as powerful reminders that in the world of digital assets, prevention truly is the best protection.

As you continue your cryptocurrency journey, remember that security should never be an afterthought. Whether you're just starting to explore digital assets or you're an experienced investor, the principles and practices outlined in this chapter will help you navigate the crypto landscape with greater confidence and security. By implementing these security measures and remaining vigilant, you're not just protecting your investments—you're helping to build a more secure and reliable cryptocurrency ecosystem for everyone.

The key takeaway from this chapter is clear: successful cryptocurrency investment requires more than just market knowledge and trading skills—it demands a comprehensive understanding of security principles and a commitment to implementing them consistently. As we move forward, let these lessons guide your approach to cryptocurrency security, ensuring that your digital assets remain protected in an increasingly complex and evolving landscape.

Chapter Nine

Tax Compliance: Understanding Crypto Regulations

The intersection of cryptocurrency and tax regulations represents one of the most challenging aspects of digital asset ownership that many investors overlook until it's too late. As governments worldwide have begun to establish clearer frameworks for cryptocurrency taxation, understanding your obligations has become not just important, but essential for anyone involved in the crypto space. As cryptocurrency moves further into the mainstream, tax authorities around the world have intensified their focus on digital asset transactions and holdings. Understanding the tax implications of cryptocurrency activities has become a crucial skill for investors who want to stay compliant while maximizing their investment potential.

The complexity of crypto taxation stems from its unique characteristics - digital assets can be bought, sold, traded, staked, or used for payments across international borders with ease. Each transaction potentially triggers tax events that need to be carefully documented and reported. Whether you're mining cryptocurrency, trading on exchanges, or using it to purchase goods and services, there are specific tax implications to consider.

Navigating these requirements can feel overwhelming at first, but with proper knowledge and systems in place, it becomes a manageable aspect of cryptocurrency investment. This chapter will break down the essential components of crypto tax compliance, from identifying taxable events to implementing effective record-keeping practices.

To underscore the importance of proper tax management, let me share River's story. River, a dedicated crypto enthusiast, learned the importance of proper tax compliance the hard way during their first year of active trading. After conducting over 200 trades across multiple platforms, they were shocked to discover they hadn't maintained adequate records for tax reporting. What followed was a three-week odyssey of piecing together transaction histories, calculating gains and losses, and consulting with tax professionals to ensure accurate reporting.

The experience taught River valuable lessons about the importance of real-time record-keeping and understanding tax obligations before engaging in crypto transactions. They now maintain a detailed spreadsheet of all crypto activities and use specialized crypto tax software to track their transactions throughout the year. This proactive approach has transformed what was once a stressful annual scramble into a manageable process, allowing River to focus on their investment strategy rather than worrying about compliance issues.

River's story reflects a common experience among cryptocurrency investors who initially underestimate the importance of tax compliance. As we explore the various aspects of cryptocurrency taxation and regulation in this chapter, you'll learn how to avoid similar pitfalls and develop robust systems for managing your tax obligations effectively.

Identifying Taxable Events in Cryptocurrency Transactions

Understanding which cryptocurrency activities trigger taxable events is crucial for maintaining compliance with tax regulations. A taxable event occurs whenever you realize a gain or loss on your cryptocurrency holdings, whether through selling, trading, or using digital assets for purchases. These events must be carefully tracked and reported to avoid potential penalties and legal issues.

One of the most common taxable events occurs when selling cryptocurrency for fiat currency. When you sell Bitcoin, Ethereum, or any other cryptocurrency for dollars, euros, or other government-issued currency, you must report any capital gains or losses based on the difference between your purchase price (cost basis) and the sale price. For instance, if you bought Bitcoin at $30,000 and sold it at $40,000, you would need to report a $10,000 capital gain.

Crypto-to-crypto exchanges also constitute taxable events, despite a common misconception among new investors. Converting one cryptocurrency to another – such as trading Bitcoin for Ethereum – is treated as if you first sold your original cryptocurrency for cash and then used that cash to purchase the new cryptocurrency. Tax authorities do not recognize like-kind exchanges for cryptocurrency transactions, meaning you cannot defer capital gains tax when swapping one digital asset for another.

Using cryptocurrency to purchase goods or services triggers a taxable event as well. The transaction is treated as if you sold your cryptocurrency at its fair market value at the time of the purchase. For example, if you use Bitcoin worth $5,000 to buy a computer, and your original cost basis for that Bitcoin was $3,000, you would need to report a $2,000 capital gain.

Mining rewards and staking income represent another category of taxable events. When you receive cryptocurrency through mining activities or as staking rewards, the fair market value of the coins at the time of receipt must be reported as ordinary income. Additionally, if you later sell these coins, you'll need to calculate capital gains or losses based on any change in value since they were received.

Airdrops and hard forks also generally constitute taxable events. When you receive new tokens through an airdrop or as a result of a blockchain fork, the fair market value of these tokens at the time of receipt is considered taxable income. This applies even if you didn't request or want the new tokens.

However, not all cryptocurrency activities trigger tax obligations. Buying cryptocurrency with fiat currency, transferring digital assets between wallets you own, or simply holding cryptocurrency without selling or trading are generally not considered taxable events. Additionally, giving cryptocurrency as a gift may not trigger an immediate tax liability for the giver, though the recipient inherits the original cost basis for future capital gains calculations.

Donating cryptocurrency to qualified charitable organizations presents a unique opportunity. Such donations may provide tax benefits, potentially allowing you to deduct the fair market value without paying capital gains tax. This can be an effective strategy for both supporting causes you care about and managing your tax obligations.

To effectively manage these various taxable events, maintaining detailed records is essential. For each transaction, you should document the date of acquisition, cost basis, date of disposal, proceeds from sale or fair market value at the time of transaction, and any associated fees. Many investors find that using specialized cryptocurrency tax software helps streamline this process and ensures accurate reporting.

Record-Keeping Requirements and Best Practices

Maintaining accurate records of cryptocurrency transactions isn't just good practice - it's a legal requirement that can save significant headaches during tax season and potential audits. The IRS requires detailed documentation of all cryptocurrency activities, including purchases, sales, trades, mining rewards, and any other transactions involving digital assets.

A robust record-keeping system should track several key elements for each transaction. These include the date and time of the transaction, the type of cryptocurrency involved, the amount of the transaction in both cryptocurrency and fiat currency terms, the fair market value at the time of the transaction, and the purpose of the transaction. Additionally, you should maintain records of the wallet addresses involved and transaction IDs that can serve as proof of the transfer on the blockchain.

One effective approach is to use specialized cryptocurrency tax software that can automatically import and track transactions across multiple exchanges and wallets. These platforms can help ensure accuracy and completeness in your records while reducing the manual effort required for documentation. However, it's important not to rely solely on third-party software - maintaining your own backup records is crucial.

When it comes to organizing your records, consider implementing a systematic approach that includes regular reconciliation of your transactions. Create separate folders or categories for different types of transactions such as trades, mining income, staking rewards, and purchases. Keep detailed spreadsheets that track your cost basis for each acquisition and maintain copies of all relevant documentation, including exchange statements and transaction confirmations.

The IRS recommends keeping cryptocurrency records for at least three years from the date you file your return or two years from the date you pay the tax, whichever is later. However, in cases where you've claimed a loss from worthless securities or bad debt deduction, records should be maintained for seven years. Given the evolving nature of cryptocurrency regulations, it's often prudent to keep records even longer.

During tax season, proper record-keeping becomes invaluable. Your records should enable you to accurately calculate gains and losses, determine holding periods for capital gains treatment, and substantiate all reported income and deductions. This includes tracking the cost basis of your cryptocurrency - the original value you paid plus any associated fees - which is essential for calculating capital gains or losses when you dispose of the assets.

For businesses accepting cryptocurrency payments, additional record-keeping requirements apply. These include maintaining records of customer transactions, recording the fair market value of cryptocurrency received as payment at the time of receipt, and tracking any fees associated with converting cryptocurrency to fiat currency. To ensure compliance and accuracy, consider implementing these best practices:

- Download and save monthly statements from all exchanges and platforms you use
- Take screenshots or maintain logs of significant transactions
- Keep detailed records of wallet addresses and private keys
- Document the methods used to determine fair market value
- Store backup copies of all records in secure, separate locations

Proper record-keeping also extends to tracking lost or stolen cryptocurrency. If you experience a loss due to theft or fraud, maintaining detailed documentation of the incident and its circumstances may help support a tax deduction claim for the loss. This includes any police reports, correspondence with exchanges or wallet providers, and evidence of the theft.

The complexity of cryptocurrency transactions makes it crucial to establish these record-keeping systems before engaging in significant trading or investment activity. Starting with good habits and maintaining them consistently will help ensure you're prepared for any future reporting requirements or audits. Remember that the burden of proof for cryptocurrency transactions lies with the taxpayer, making comprehensive record-keeping not just helpful, but essential for legal compliance.

International Compliance and Cross-Border Considerations

The global nature of cryptocurrency presents unique challenges when it comes to regulatory compliance across different jurisdictions. As we approach 2025, the cryptocurrency regulatory environment remains highly fragmented, with different countries implementing varied frameworks ranging from highly supportive to restrictive. This lack of unified global approach creates significant complexity for individuals and businesses operating across borders.

Currently, approximately 62% of Financial Stability Board (FSB) members are working toward regulatory alignment for crypto-assets, with a similar percentage focusing on stablecoin regulations. However, substantial gaps persist as many service providers continue to operate without robust regulation or in non-compliance with applicable jurisdictional rules. This regulatory patchwork means that cryptocurrency users must carefully navigate multiple, sometimes conflicting, regulatory requirements when conducting international transactions.

The United States, for instance, still lacks a comprehensive regulatory framework for cryptocurrencies, though significant legislation has been introduced. Other jurisdictions have taken varying approaches, from creating crypto-friendly environments to implementing strict controls on digital asset transactions. This diversity in regulatory approaches creates challenges for users engaging in cross-border activities, as a transaction that is fully compliant in one country may violate regulations in another.

Stablecoins face particularly intense scrutiny in the international arena due to their potential vulnerability to sudden loss of confidence and runs on the issuer or underlying reserve assets. Regulatory authorities worldwide are working to establish specific requirements addressing these vulnerabilities, especially in cross-border contexts.

This heightened attention to stablecoins reflects growing concern about their potential impact on financial stability.

For cryptocurrency users engaged in international transactions, implementing robust compliance strategies is essential. This includes maintaining comprehensive documentation of all cross-border activities, understanding tax obligations in multiple jurisdictions, and conducting thorough due diligence on any international trading partners or service providers. Users must also stay informed about regulatory developments across relevant jurisdictions, as the landscape continues to evolve rapidly.

Data management requirements present another layer of complexity in cross-border compliance. With the increasing adoption of blockchain and tokenization, authorities are implementing stricter requirements for data accuracy, storage, and management. These requirements vary by jurisdiction, creating additional compliance burdens for international operators. Users must ensure their record-keeping practices satisfy the most stringent applicable standards to maintain compliance across all relevant jurisdictions.

Looking ahead, several key trends are shaping the future of international cryptocurrency compliance. There is a growing emphasis on harmonizing regulatory approaches across jurisdictions, though complete uniformity remains a distant goal. Consumer protection is receiving increased attention, with regulators focusing on protecting retail investors from fraud, market manipulation, and other risks.

Additionally, regulatory scrutiny of offshore operations is intensifying, with authorities paying closer attention to crypto businesses operating from jurisdictions with minimal oversight.

To navigate this complex landscape effectively, cryptocurrency users should adopt a comprehensive approach to international compliance. This includes implementing robust documentation practices, maintaining accurate records of all cross-border transactions, and regularly monitoring regulatory developments in relevant jurisdictions. Users should also consider working with qualified legal and tax professionals who understand the nuances of cryptocurrency regulation in different jurisdictions.

The path toward clear and comprehensive global cryptocurrency regulation continues to develop, with efforts toward greater international coordination gaining momentum. While complete regulatory harmony may be years away, the trend is moving toward more consistent approaches to digital asset regulation across borders. This evolution presents both challenges and opportunities for cryptocurrency users, making it essential to stay informed and maintain adaptable compliance strategies. As we conclude our exploration of cryptocurrency taxation and regulatory compliance, it's clear that understanding and adhering to tax obligations is a fundamental aspect of responsible digital asset ownership. The landscape of cryptocurrency regulation continues to evolve, making it essential for investors to remain informed and adaptable in their approach to compliance.

River's story serves as a powerful reminder that proactive tax management is far more effective than reactive scrambling. Their journey from tax confusion to organized compliance mirrors the path many cryptocurrency investors must take. By implementing proper record-keeping systems, staying informed about regulatory requirements, and maintaining detailed transaction histories, investors can transform tax compliance from a daunting challenge into a manageable routine.

The key takeaways from this chapter emphasize several critical points. First, understanding taxable events is crucial - whether trading, mining, or using cryptocurrency for purchases, each action may have tax implications that require proper documentation. Second, maintaining comprehensive records isn't just good practice; it's a legal requirement that can protect you during audits and ensure accurate reporting. Finally, for those operating internationally, awareness of cross-border regulations and compliance requirements is essential for navigating the global cryptocurrency landscape.

As we move forward in the cryptocurrency space, tax compliance will likely become even more structured and regulated. The strategies and systems we've discussed in this chapter provide a foundation for managing these obligations effectively. Remember that staying compliant isn't only about avoiding penalties – it's about contributing to the legitimacy and maturation of the cryptocurrency ecosystem as a whole.

By implementing the practices and principles covered in this chapter, you're not just protecting yourself from potential legal issues; you're positioning yourself to take full advantage of the opportunities that cryptocurrency offers while maintaining peace of mind about your tax obligations. As we transition to our final chapter on the future of cryptocurrency, we carry forward the understanding that proper tax compliance is an integral part of successful cryptocurrency investment and usage.

Chapter Ten

Future Horizons: The Evolving Cryptocurrency Landscape

The cryptocurrency landscape stands at a fascinating crossroads where innovation meets regulation, and possibility converges with practicality. As we peer into the horizon of digital finance, we find ourselves witnessing the early stages of a technological renaissance that promises to reshape our understanding of value exchange and financial systems. The transformative power of blockchain technology and cryptocurrencies extends far beyond their current applications, promising to reshape industries from finance and healthcare to supply chain management and digital identity. As we stand at this pivotal moment, witnessing the convergence of traditional financial systems with innovative digital solutions, it's crucial to understand the emerging trends and potential developments that will shape our financial future.

The rise of Central Bank Digital Currencies (CBDCs) represents one of the most significant developments in this evolution, with major economies worldwide exploring and implementing their own digital currency projects. This transition marks a fascinating intersection between centralized authority and decentralized technology, potentially bridging the gap between traditional banking and the crypto ecosystem.

During a recent cryptocurrency conference, I met Poppy, a climate scientist turned blockchain developer, who shared a compelling story about her journey into sustainable cryptocurrency mining. She had initially been skeptical of cryptocurrency due to its energy consumption, but rather than dismissing the technology entirely, she decided to tackle the problem head-on. Poppy developed a small-scale mining operation powered entirely by solar energy in her backyard. What started as an experiment soon turned into a proof of concept that attracted attention from local tech enthusiasts. She documented every step, from the initial set-up challenges to the final successful implementation, creating a blueprint for others to follow. Her story perfectly illustrates how innovation in the cryptocurrency space isn't just about financial technology - it's about finding creative solutions to real-world problems and building a more sustainable future for digital assets. Through Poppy's experience, we can see how individual initiatives can contribute to the broader evolution of cryptocurrency infrastructure, making it more environmentally conscious and sustainable for future generations.

As we delve into the future horizons of cryptocurrency, we'll explore not just the technological innovations on the horizon, but also the practical implications these developments have for investors, businesses, and everyday users. From the evolution of decentralized finance (DeFi) to the emerging Web3 ecosystem, understanding these trends is crucial for anyone looking to navigate the future of digital assets effectively.

The integration of blockchain technology into our daily lives continues to accelerate, with applications extending far beyond simple financial transactions. Smart contracts are automating complex processes, while tokenization is creating new forms of digital ownership and value exchange. These developments are laying the groundwork for a more inclusive and efficient financial system, though not without their own unique challenges and considerations.

The Rise of Central Bank Digital Currencies (CBDCs) and Their Impact

The emergence of Central Bank Digital Currencies (CBDCs) represents a watershed moment in the evolution of money, marking a significant shift in how governments and financial institutions approach digital assets. As traditional banking systems adapt to the digital age, central banks worldwide are actively exploring or implementing their own digital currencies, creating a new paradigm that bridges conventional monetary policy with technological innovation.

Unlike decentralized cryptocurrencies, CBDCs are government-backed digital currencies issued and regulated directly by national central banks. They function as the digital equivalent of physical cash, maintaining the same value and government guarantees that support traditional fiat currency. This fundamental difference sets them apart from private cryptocurrencies, as CBDCs operate within existing monetary frameworks while leveraging the efficiency and accessibility of digital technology.

The global landscape of CBDC development showcases varying levels of progress and implementation. The Bahamas made history with the Sand Dollar, one of the first fully operational retail CBDCs, while China's Digital Yuan (e-CNY) continues extensive testing across major metropolitan areas. The European Central Bank has advanced its digital euro project through various testing phases, and numerous other nations are actively researching or piloting their own CBDC initiatives.

The potential benefits of CBDCs extend far beyond simple digitization of currency. They promise to enhance financial inclusion by providing banking-like services to underserved populations, particularly in regions with limited traditional banking infrastructure. CBDCs could significantly reduce transaction costs, especially for cross-border payments and remittances, while simplifying the implementation of monetary and fiscal policies through more direct transmission mechanisms.

However, the rise of CBDCs also presents significant challenges and concerns. Privacy implications remain a central issue, as the direct visibility of financial transactions by government authorities raises important questions about personal privacy and financial surveillance. Technical challenges around system resilience, security, and universal accessibility must be addressed, while the potential disruption to traditional banking models and deposit systems requires careful consideration.

The relationship between CBDCs and existing cryptocurrencies highlights a complex dynamic in the evolving digital currency landscape. While both represent forms of digital money, their fundamental differences in governance, value stability, and underlying philosophy suggest a future where multiple forms of digital currency might coexist, each serving distinct purposes within the broader financial ecosystem.

As CBDCs continue to develop, international coordination and standardization become increasingly important. The lack of unified standards could create interoperability challenges between different CBDC systems, while geopolitical considerations influence development priorities and implementation strategies. The future may see the emergence of international frameworks governing CBDC interactions, potentially reshaping global financial flows and monetary sovereignty.

The impact of CBDCs extends beyond mere technological innovation – they represent a fundamental shift in how we conceptualize and interact with money. As these systems mature, they have the potential to transform payment systems, enhance financial inclusion, and redefine the relationship between central banks, financial institutions, and the general public. Understanding these developments becomes crucial for anyone interested in the future of finance and digital currency.

Environmental Sustainability and Green Blockchain Solutions

The environmental impact of cryptocurrency has become one of the most pressing challenges facing the digital asset industry. As blockchain technology continues to evolve, the massive energy consumption associated with cryptocurrency mining, particularly Bitcoin, has raised significant concerns about sustainability and environmental responsibility. The scale of this impact is staggering - Bitcoin networks alone consume more electricity than several developed countries, including Norway and Sweden, with a carbon footprint equivalent to burning 38 billion tons of coal.

The environmental toll extends far beyond carbon emissions. The water footprint of Bitcoin mining operations would have met the domestic water needs of more than 300 million people in sub-Saharan Africa. Mining facilities require substantial physical space, generate significant noise pollution, and contribute to growing electronic waste problems as mining hardware rapidly becomes obsolete. These environmental consequences have prompted economists and environmentalists to question whether the benefits of cryptocurrency mining outweigh its environmental costs.

However, the cryptocurrency industry is actively responding to these challenges through various innovative solutions and commitments to sustainability. A significant shift is occurring as the industry pivots away from energy-intensive proof-of-work systems toward more sustainable alternatives. Proof-of-stake mechanisms, which require significantly less energy than traditional mining, are gaining prominence as a more environmentally conscious approach to blockchain validation.

The emergence of carbon-neutral cryptocurrencies represents another promising development in the quest for sustainability. This transformation is being driven by multiple factors, including growing environmental awareness, increasing regulatory scrutiny, and rising demand from environmentally conscious investors and consumers. Many mining operations are now transitioning to renewable energy sources, incorporating solar, wind, and hydroelectric power into their operations.

The environmental impact of cryptocurrency mining has also raised important public health considerations. Research has demonstrated a direct link between Bitcoin mining operations and increased levels of harmful air pollution, adding another dimension to the urgency of developing sustainable solutions. This connection between cryptocurrency's carbon footprint and public health outcomes has strengthened the case for immediate action toward greener practices.

For investors focused on Environmental, Social, and Governance (ESG) criteria, the environmental challenges of cryptocurrency present a significant concern. The relative lack of comprehensive regulations around crypto activities has complicated efforts to address these environmental impacts, though this regulatory landscape is evolving as digital currencies become increasingly mainstream. The industry's commitment to decarbonization by 2025 represents a crucial step, but progress toward this goal has been uneven.

The push toward sustainable blockchain solutions isn't merely a trend – it's increasingly recognized as essential for the long-term viability of the cryptocurrency ecosystem. As public awareness grows and regulatory pressure intensifies, the ability to demonstrate environmental responsibility will likely become a crucial factor in determining which cryptocurrencies and blockchain projects succeed in the future. The industry's challenge lies in balancing innovation and growth with environmental stewardship, ensuring that the financial opportunities created by digital currencies don't come at the expense of our planet's health.

The development of green blockchain solutions represents a critical evolution in cryptocurrency's journey toward mainstream adoption. By addressing environmental concerns head-on through technological innovation and industry-wide commitments to sustainability, the cryptocurrency sector is working to ensure its role in the future of finance aligns with global environmental goals. This transformation demonstrates how technological innovation can adapt to meet environmental challenges while maintaining the revolutionary potential of blockchain technology.

Web3 and the Integration of Digital Assets in Daily Life

The integration of digital assets into daily life represents one of the most transformative aspects of the Web3 revolution. As blockchain technology evolves beyond its financial origins, we're witnessing the emergence of a new digital ecosystem where cryptocurrencies, NFTs, and tokenized assets are becoming increasingly woven into the fabric of everyday experiences. This shift isn't just about new ways to transact – it's fundamentally changing how we interact with digital services, manage our identities, and participate in the digital economy.

At its core, Web3 represents a paradigm shift from the centralized platforms that dominated the previous era of the internet. Unlike traditional web services where users surrender control of their data and digital assets to corporate intermediaries, Web3 empowers individuals to maintain sovereignty over their digital presence through decentralized applications (dApps) and smart contracts. This new architecture is enabling novel forms of digital ownership and interaction that were previously impossible.

The practical implementation of Web3 technologies is rapidly expanding across various sectors. Digital wallets have evolved beyond simple cryptocurrency storage to become comprehensive gateways for accessing decentralized services. These wallets now serve as digital identity hubs, allowing users to authenticate themselves across platforms, manage their digital assets, and participate in decentralized governance systems. The integration of payment tools and

APIs has made it increasingly seamless for businesses to incorporate cryptocurrency transactions into their operations, bridging the gap between traditional commerce and the digital asset economy.

Decentralized Finance (DeFi) protocols have emerged as a powerful demonstration of Web3's potential to transform financial services. These protocols provide access to lending, borrowing, and yield-generating opportunities without requiring traditional bank accounts or credit scores. This democratization of financial services is particularly significant for underserved populations who have historically faced barriers to accessing conventional banking systems.

The convergence of artificial intelligence with blockchain technology is creating even more sophisticated possibilities for digital asset integration. AI-powered interfaces are making Web3 services more intuitive and accessible, while blockchain's transparent audit trails address concerns about AI accountability. This combination enables the development of autonomous agents capable of executing complex transactions on behalf of users while maintaining transparency and trust.

However, the path to widespread adoption faces significant challenges. Despite technological advances, many Web3 platforms still primarily cater to developers and crypto enthusiasts rather than mainstream users. The need for more intuitive interfaces and robust support tools remains crucial for broader adoption. Additionally, regulatory uncertainty continues to pose challenges, particularly in the banking sector where a majority of Web3 firms face difficulties establishing traditional banking relationship.

Privacy considerations also present a unique challenge in the Web3 ecosystem. While public blockchains offer unprecedented transparency, this can conflict with privacy requirements, especially as AI systems require extensive datasets for training. The development of privacy-preserving technologies like zero-knowledge proofs represents an important frontier in addressing these concerns while maintaining the benefits of decentralization.

As we look toward the future, the integration of digital assets through Web3 technologies continues to accelerate, driven by real-world incentives and practical applications. Decentralized physical infrastructure networks (DePIN) are demonstrating the potential for blockchain technology to coordinate and incentivize the development of real-world infrastructure[107], while new tools and frameworks are making it easier for developers to build user-friendly decentralized applications.

The transformation brought about by Web3 and digital assets represents more than just technological innovation - it's a fundamental shift in how we conceptualize and interact with digital value. As these systems mature and overcome current challenges, they have the potential to create a more inclusive, transparent, and user-controlled digital economy. The key to realizing this potential lies in continuing to develop solutions that balance technological sophistication with practical usability, ensuring that the benefits of Web3 become accessible to everyone, not just technical experts.

As we conclude our exploration of cryptocurrency's future horizons, it's clear that we stand at the threshold of a transformative era in digital finance. The convergence of CBDCs, sustainable blockchain solutions, and Web3 technologies isn't just reshaping how we think about money - it's fundamentally changing how we interact with value in the digital age. Poppy's story of sustainable mining innovation perfectly encapsulates the spirit of this evolution. Her journey from skeptic to pioneer demonstrates how individual initiative and creative problem-solving can address even the most challenging aspects of cryptocurrency adoption. As more innovators like Poppy step forward, we're seeing the emergence of solutions that balance technological advancement with environmental responsibility.

The rise of CBDCs represents perhaps the most significant institutional acknowledgment of digital currency's potential, while developments in green blockchain technology are addressing crucial environmental concerns. Meanwhile, Web3's integration into daily life continues to expand the possibilities for how we use and interact with digital assets.

Yet, as we've explored throughout this book, the future of cryptocurrency isn't only about technological innovation -

it's about creating a more inclusive, sustainable, and accessible financial system. The challenges ahead are significant, from regulatory uncertainties to environmental concerns, but the opportunities for positive change are equally compelling.

As you continue your journey in the cryptocurrency space, remember that knowledge and adaptability are your greatest assets. Stay informed about emerging trends, remain vigilant about security, and always approach new developments with a balanced perspective of both opportunities and risks. The cryptocurrency landscape will undoubtedly continue to evolve, but the fundamental principles we've discussed - from security best practices to risk management strategies - will serve as your foundation for navigating whatever changes lie ahead.

Your journey into cryptocurrency doesn't end with this book - in many ways, it's just the beginning. As you move forward, leverage the knowledge and insights you've gained to make informed decisions about your involvement in this dynamic space. Whether you're an investor, developer, or simply someone interested in the future of finance, your understanding of these fundamental concepts will help you participate meaningfully in shaping the future of digital currency.

Remember that the most successful participants in the cryptocurrency ecosystem are those who maintain a learning mindset, staying curious and adaptable as technology continues to evolve. The future of cryptocurrency is being written not just by major institutions and developers, but by everyday users who understand its potential and actively engage with its development.

As we look to the horizon, the possibilities for cryptocurrency and blockchain technology seem boundless. While we can't predict exactly how this technology will transform our world, we can be certain that understanding its fundamental principles will be crucial for navigating the financial landscape of tomorrow. Keep learning, stay vigilant, and remain engaged with this evolving ecosystem - the future of finance is digital, and you're now equipped to be part of its development.

Conclusion

Throughout our journey exploring the transformative world of cryptocurrency, we've witnessed how this innovative technology is reshaping our understanding of money, value, and financial systems. From our opening story of Sienna discovering ancient coins in Greece to Poppy's pioneering work in sustainable crypto mining, we've seen how cryptocurrency represents both a continuation of money's evolution and a revolutionary leap forward.

The ten steps we've covered in this guide have laid a foundation for understanding and engaging with digital currencies confidently and securely. We began by tracing money's evolution from physical coins to digital assets, understanding how blockchain technology provides the secure backbone for this transformation. Through practical explorations of wallets, exchanges, and investment strategies, we've equipped ourselves with the tools needed to participate in this digital financial revolution safely and intelligently.

Perhaps most importantly, we've learned that success in the cryptocurrency space isn't only about technical knowledge or trading prowess - it's about developing a comprehensive understanding that encompasses security, risk management, and regulatory compliance. The stories of individuals like Leah, who transformed cryptocurrency concepts into teachable moments, and River, who learned the critical importance of proper tax documentation, remind us that every challenge in this space presents an opportunity for growth and learning.

As we look toward the future horizons of cryptocurrency, it's clear that we're still in the early stages of this technological renaissance. The emergence of Central Bank Digital Currencies, the growing emphasis on sustainable blockchain solutions, and the integration of digital assets into daily life through Web3 technologies suggest that the innovations we've explored are just the beginning.

Remember that your cryptocurrency journey doesn't end with the completion of this guide. The landscape continues to evolve, presenting new opportunities and challenges. Stay curious, remain vigilant about security, and keep building upon the foundation we've established. Whether you're taking your first steps into crypto investing or expanding your existing knowledge, the key principles we've covered - understanding, security, compliance, and strategic thinking - will serve as your compass in navigating this dynamic digital frontier.

As we conclude our exploration, let's carry forward the lessons learned from each chapter, from the importance of proper wallet security to the necessity of maintaining detailed records for tax compliance. Your success in the cryptocurrency space will be determined not just by what you know, but by how well you implement these practices in your daily interactions with digital assets.

The future of finance is being written in the language of cryptocurrency, and you now have the tools to be an active participant in this transformation. Stay informed, remain skeptical of too-good-to-be-true promises, and always prioritize security in your crypto journey. The road ahead is exciting, and with the knowledge you've gained, you're well-equipped to navigate it with confidence and insight. Go forth and conquer!

References

Adams, R. (2025, March 21). *Your crypto tax guide.* TurboTax.

Algorand Foundation. (2024, February 1). *A guide to wallet security & best practices.* Algorand.

Amazon.com, Inc. (2014, December 31). *Enter the characters you see below.* Amazon.com.

AnalystPrep. (2023, December 12). The crypto ecosystem: Key elements and risks. AnalystPrep.

Arkose Labs. (2023). Guide to cryptocurrency security. Arkose Labs.

Barney, N., Troy, S., & Pratt, M. K. (2023, September 07). *What is distributed ledger technology (DLT)*? TechTarget SearchCIO.

Bedawala, M. (2023, January 17). What are Consensus Mechanisms? Visa.

Belegu, L. (2024, December). *Crypto wallet security explained: A practical guide for all Learners.* CSTA.

Bessala, J. (2024, January 01). *The crypto industry was supposed to decarbonize by 2025 - how's that* going? Corporate Knights.

Binance News. (2025, January 29). *Web3 faces challenges in expanding user base in 2025.* Binance Square.

Bitcoin.com. (2025, May 27). *How to backup and restore a crypto wallet.* Bitcoin.com.

Blackstone T. & Turner G. (2025, February 18). *2025 guide: Everything you should know to invest in crypto safely.* Security.org.

Bondarev, A. (2025, April 22). *AI meets Web3: A high-tech convergence in 2025.* Yellow.

Brooks, M. (2024, December 19). *Crypto taxes: The complete guide (2025).* CoinLedger.

Brownstein, M. (2025, April 24). *Bitcoin mining increases levels of air pollution harmful to human health.* Harvard T.H. Chan School of Public Health.

bwuser10000. (2023, March). *Best practices for storing Cryptocurrency pins, seeds, etc.* Bitwarden Community Forum.

Caleb & Brown. (2025, January 2). *Crypto portfolio basics: The key to a well-balanced portfolio in 2025.* Caleb & Brown.

California Department of Financial Protection and Innovation. (2024, July). *Crypto scams: how to avoid becoming a victim.* DFPI – California Department of Financial Protection and Innovation.

CFI Team. (2022, November). *Cryptocurrency exchanges.* Corporate Finance Institute.

CFI Team. (2023). *Cryptocurrency wallet.* Corporate Finance Institute.

Chakos, H. (2023, October 31). *Crypto made easy: A beginner's guide to digital asset Investments.* Apple Books.

Chimienti M. T., Kochanska U., Pinna A. (2019, May). *Understanding the crypto-asset phenomenon, its risks and measurement issues.* European Central Bank.

Chronister A. (2022, September 27). History of the barter system? Prime Trade NW.

Coinbase. (2024). *Understanding crypto taxes.* Coinbase Learn.

CoinCover.(2025, April 24). *Developing resilient crypto wallets: security best practices for developers.* CoinCover.

CoinDCX.(2023, October 4). *Top 10 books on blockchain & crypto: A beginner's guide.* CoinDCX Blog.

Coursera Staff. (2025, January 22). *How to trade cryptocurrency: A practical guide for beginners.* Coursera.

Crust Lab. (2023, December 15). *What is a crypto ecosystem: Key components, risks and functions.* Crust Lab.

Cryptohopper. (2023). *Crypto trading 101: Trading strategies for beginners.* Cryptohopper.

Cryptopedia Staff. (2025, February 26). *A Beginner's Guide to Day Trading Crypto.* Gemini Cryptopedia.

Deloitte Luxembourg. (2023). Blockchain - distributed ledger technology: A stitch intime. Deloitte Luxembourg.

Doss R. (2025, January 29). *How to avoid the most common cryptocurrency scams.* Government Technology.

Fairview, D. (2024, November 16). *Bitcoin and cryptocurrency made easy: A step-by-step guide to understanding, buying, and profiting from crypto – Secure your financial future with Sim.* Liberty Bay Books.

Federal Reserve Board. (2024, August 2). *Central bank digital currency (CBDC).* Federal Reserve.

Fidelity Investments. (2025, April 02). *2025 crypto regulatory outlook.* Fidelity.

FINNY team. (2024, November 25). *A guide to diversifying your crypto portfolio with alternative investments.* FINNY.

F-Secure. (2025, March 23). *How to identify and avoid crypto scams.* F-Secure.

Garnett, A. G. (2023). *Diversifying your crypto portfolio: A complete guide.* Honey Bricks.

Hacken. (2025, April 15). Consensus mechanisms in blockchain: A deep dive into the different types. Hacken.

Hackers Tent Recovery Service. (2025, April 8). *2025 guide to verified crypto recovery services.* Infosecurity Magazine.

Hedera. (2024, March 1). What are distributed ledger technologies (DLTs)? Hedera Learning Center.

Hetler, A. (2024, December 17). *Common cryptocurrency scams.* TechTarget.

Howitt, D. (2019). *What is classed as a taxable event for* cryptocurrencies? Recap Help Center.

Hyman, V. (2025, February 6). *Your guide to understanding CBDCs.* Mastercard News.

Internal Revenue Service. (2024, April). *Taxpayers need to report crypto, other digital asset transactions on their tax return.* IRS.gov.

Internal Revenue Service. (2025, April 23). *Digital assets.* IRS.gov.

Investopedia. (2024). *How to choose a cryptocurrency exchange.* Investopedia.

Investopedia. (2024). What are consensus mechanisms in blockchain and cryptocurrency? Investopedia.

Investopedia. (2024, February 07). History of money: From bartering to digital currency. Investopedia.

Investopedia. (2024, March 15). Blockchain facts: What is it, how it works, and how it can be used. Investopedia.

Investopedia Staff. (2024, March). *Central bank digital currency (CBDC): Definition, types, and examples.* Investopedia.

Investopedia. (2024). *Distributed ledger technology (DLT): What it is, how it works.* Investopedia.

Investopedia. (2025, May). *What is a cryptocurrency wallet? Types and how to choose.* Investopedia.

Janeau, E. (2023, November 21). The barter system: Definition & examples. Study.com.

Kamen S. & Angel M. (2024, May 22). *New Crypto Reporting Will Require Rigorous Recordkeeping.* Holland & Knight LLP.

Kaspersky. (2023). *How to Strengthen your Cryptocurrency* Security? Kaspersky Resource Center.

Kraken Learn team. (2024, November 19). *How do cryptocurrencies use* cryptography? Kraken.

Kraken Learn team. (2025, February 4). What is a blockchain consensus mechanism? Kraken.

Kraken Learn team. (2025, February 24). *Crypto trading strategies you need to know*. Kraken Learn.

Kriptomat. (2023, December). *How to build a balanced crypto portfolio: Strategies for risk diversification*. Kriptomat.

Kubiak, I. (2025, April 26). *Digital gold? UNM economics professors help decode the high cost of Bitcoin mining.* UNM News.

Labonte, M. & Nelson, R. M. (2025, April 10). *Central bank digital currencies.* Congressional Research Service.

La Rédaction C. (2023, July). *Ultimate guide to Bitcoin wallet Backup: Step-by-step instructions.* Cointribune.

Law Offices of Sammy Kim. (2024, September). *Taxable events in the crypto world: What triggers a tax obligation?* VA Tax Attorney.

Ledger. (2023, September 13). Consensus mechanisms: How blockchains stay secure. Ledger Academy.

Levy, G. (2025, May). Blockchain and Bitcoin fundamentals. Udemy.

Lodhi, N. (2025, March 17). *Crypto taxes: Your ultimate guide.* ezTaxReturn.

Miller, F. (2023). *Crypto Master: The ultimate beginner's guide to cryptocurrency trading and investing.* Walmart.com.

Muller, M. (2025). *How to keep your crypto secure.* Coinbase.

Musiala Jr., R. A. (2025, February 18). *Weekly blockchain blog - Feb. 17, 2025.* Baker Law.

Nair, V. (2025, January 9). *What Are the Different Types of Crypto* Wallets? Ledger Academy.

Onchain Research Team. (2024, January 01). *The world needs DePIN. Not the Web3 world. The entire* world. Onchain.

OSL. (2025, April 16). *The rise of carbon-neutral cryptocurrencies in 2025.* OSL Academy.

OSL. (2025, April 16). *The growing need for clear crypto regulations in 2025.* OSL Academy.

PwC. (2024, March 11). *Understanding cryptocurrency and digital assets.* PwC US.

RCI Bank. (2024, September 04). The evolution of money: From barter to bank notes and beyond. Bank UK.

Reserve Bank of Australia. (2022, January 01). *Digital currencies.* Reserve Bank of Australia.

Richardson, D. (2023, November 23). *The 5 crypto trading strategies that every trader needs to know.* IG.

Schöllauf, P. (2025, March 10). Bitcoin's history & evolution: From Cypherpunks to cryptographic milestones. Blockpit.

Scottsdale Mint. (2025, January 17). *CBDC explained: What is a central bank digital currency? (Complete 2025 guide).* Scottsdale Mint.

Sebastian. (2022, April 8). Timeline of cryptocurrencies. Timelines.

Sethi, R. (2024, November 23). *Portfolio rebalancing: What it really means & how to do it.* I will teach you to be rich.

Shafii, K. (2023, November 20). Blockchain vs. DLT (distributed ledger technology) explained. Consensus.

Shardeum Content Team. (2023, March 1). *Understanding blockchain architecture: A comprehensive guide.* Shardeum.

Shrimpy Team. (2023, May 08). *What is portfolio* rebalancing? Shrimpy Academy.

Singh, D. (2024, October 21). *Key Components of a Blockchain Explained: Unlocking Blockchain's Potential.* Debut Infotech.

Singh, D. (2025, January 21). *Crypto Exchange Security: Building Trust in Centralized Platforms.* Debut Infotech.

Solanki, S. (2025, March 21). *Cryptocurrency laws and regulations.* Thomson Reuters Legal.

Sponsored. (2025, May 15). *Best crypto tools to integrate into your Web3 project in 2025.* The Tribune.

tastylive. (2023, March 13). *3 types of crypto wallets for beginners.* tastylive.

Team CoinSwitch. (2023, July 19). *The three different types of cryptocurrency exchanges: CEXs, DEXs, and hybrid exchanges*. CoinSwitch.

Telcoin. (2024). *Types of cryptocurrency wallet*. Telco.in.

Thaxton, R. (2023, May 18). The history of money: from silver coins to credit cards.FOREX.com.

The Luxury Playbook. (2025, May 15). *How to backup your crypto wallet (Step-by-step guide & tips)*. The Luxury Playbook.

Token Metrics Team. (2024). *Portfolio diversification - What it is and how to diversify crypto investments?* Token Metrics.

Trakx. (2024, September 23). *Crypto security: Best practices to protect digital assets*. Trakx.

Vault12 Inc. (2025). *How to back up crypto wallet*. Vault12.

Wadhwani K. (2023, September). *Enhancing security in cryptocurrency wallets: Best practices and emerging Technologies*. SoluLab.

WazirX Content Team. (2023, December 7). *Crypto portfolio rebalancing: Strategies, benefits, and risks*. WazirX.

Weston, G. (2024, December 16). *What is blockchain architecture? A beginner's guide to the basics*. 101 Blockchains.

Wikipediacontributors. (2024, April 24). Cryptocurrency. Wikipedia.

Wunder Trading. (2025, January 10). *5 different types of cryptocurrency exchanges: Understanding crypto trading platforms*. Wunder Trading Journal.

About the Author

Bruno Steele

A passionate advocate for financial innovation who discovered cryptocurrency in its early days and spent years exploring its transformative potential. Drawing from real-world experience in trading, investing, and navigating the evolving crypto landscape, the author has helped many newcomers understand digital currencies through educational content and community workshops. When not writing or researching blockchain technology, they can be found mentoring lifelong learners dedicated to making complex topics simple and accessible. Bruno believes that everyone deserves the tools to take control of their financial future—regardless of their technical background. Known for his clear explanations, practical insights, and relatable teaching style, Bruno empowers everyday individuals to confidently explore cryptocurrency and blockchain technology. His mission is to break down barriers, bust myths, and help readers navigate the digital economy with confidence and care.

Note to Readers:

Please take a minute to leave a review. It would be appreciated and essential for like-minded readers to discover the book too. Thank you.

www.ingramcontent.com/pod-product-compliance
Lightning Source LLC
LaVergne TN
LVHW022050200926
848481LV00003B/845
* 9 7 9 8 3 4 9 4 3 6 7 6 5 *